LOST ATLANTIS

James Bramwell

npc

NEWCASTLE PUBLISHING COMPANY, INC.
1521 No. Vine St.   Hollywood, Calif. 90028

A NEWCASTLE BOOK
FIRST PRINTING: MARCH 1974
PRINTED IN THE UNITED STATES OF AMERICA

ACKNOWLEDGMENTS

The Author's acknowledgments and thanks are due to the following. To Mr Duncan Wilson for criticisms and suggestions on the chapter, *The Story of Atlantis*. To Mr Lewis Spence for permission to quote extensively from his works, and to Messrs Rider. To Professor Taylor and Messrs Methuen for the use of the translation of the *Timaeus* and *Critias*. To the editors of the Loeb Classical Library for a portion of Professor Oldfather's translation of *Diodorus Siculus*. To Mr H. S. Bellamy and Messrs Faber and Faber for the extract from *Moons, Myths, and Man* on Glacial Cosmogony. To Mrs Frieda Lawrence and Messrs William Heinemann for the quotations from *Birds, Beasts, and Flowers*, and from *The Plumed Serpent*. To Mr John Masefield and Messrs Heinemann for the stanzas from *Fragments* in the *Collected Poems of John Masefield*. To Mr L. H. Myers and Messrs Jonathan Cape for the extract from *The Root and the Flower*. To Senator W. B. Yeats and Messrs Macmillan for the quotation from *The Indian To His Lover* and from *The Secret Rose*. To Mr G. C. Macaulay and Messrs Macmillan for the extract from the translation of *Herodotus*. To Mr C. Day Lewis and the Hogarth Press for the quotation from *From Feathers to Iron*. To Mr Wyndham Lewis and Messrs Faber and Faber for the quotation from *One Way Song*. To Mr Wilson Knight and Messrs Dent for the quotation from *Atlantic Crossing*. And to Messrs Frederic Muller for the quotations from Count Kuhn de Prorok's *In Search of Lost Worlds*.

Acknowledgments and thanks are also due to Herr Leo Frobenius and to Dr F. Gidon, and his publishers Messrs Payot, for passages translated from their works; and to Herr Alexander Bessmertny, whose book *Das Atlantis Rätsel* is of permanent value in the objective approach to the study of Atlantis.

CONTENTS

In some green island of the sea
Where now the shadowy coral grows
In pride and pomp and empery
The courts of old Atlantis rose.

JOHN MASEFIELD

Queequeg was a native of Kokovoko, an island far away
to the west and south. It is not on any map; true places
never are.

HERMAN MELVILLE.

INTRODUCTION

The name Atlantis has a sad sound. If it is pronounced ringingly, giving the first two syllables their full consonantal resonance and allowing the final sibilant to fall softly from the tongue, the effect seems to evoke an image of the surge and hiss of huge waves breaking over submerged rocks to spend themselves in white ocean foam. Atlantis is a grand name, majestic and solemn-sounding like the opening bars of Debussy's *La Cathédrale Engloutie*, and it contains in its associations with the Atlas mountains and the Atlantic Ocean the colossal reflection of the Titan, the son of Oceanides, supporting the heavens upon his shoulders.

The tradition of Atlantis is as old, perhaps, as the hills, and because the flood-theme pervades the folk-lore and literature of every race of the world, it still retains its magic in the present day. The magic lies in the supposed antiquity of the tradition as much as in the poetry of the idea; and there are few people who can call it to mind without experiencing some emotion, whether wonder or impatience. For some, Atlantis is no more than a vague romantic symbol, a mirage perceived in that twilight state of mind which has immortal longings. There is nothing to remind one of the real world in the strange Otherworld of Atlantis as conceived by those who live on Vision.

Introduction

It is like Poe's

> strange city lying alone
> Far down in the dim West
> Where the good and the bad, and the worst and the best
> Have gone to their eternal rest,
> Where shrines and palaces and towers
> Resemble nothing that is ours . . .

or perhaps it suggests the more personal escape at the end of a love-story, an escape that is at the same time a goal . . .

> Here will we moor our lonely ship
> And wander for ever with woven hands,
> Murmuring softly lip to lip,
> Along the grass, along the sands,
> Murmuring how far away are the unquiet lands;

But for others, less romantic and more learned, the potent magic of Atlantis is a force to be counteracted; they must needs break the spell and face the fact that Isles of the Blessed and Fortunate Isles have no place in the modern world, except in the limbo of encyclopaedias and collections of fables reserved for popular legends.

And so arises the "problem," and the magic is forgotten in the hurly-burly of controversy.

What was Atlantis? Most people have heard of the island-continent which, according to ancient tradition, was engulfed by the ocean; but they are pretty hazy about its geographical position and the date of its submergence.

Did Atlantis really exist? Another question which most people would hesitate to answer, though they would probably feel an impulse to reply in the affirmative without

having any particular reason except a vague memory of
having read about it somewhere.

These are the first questions which anyone who becomes
interested in Atlantis feels bound to answer. They constitute in effect the "problem of Atlantis." Unfortunately.
For they cannot definitely be answered; or rather, they have
been answered so often and so differently that nothing
definite emerges except the necessity for keeping an open
mind about the important issues.

This initial difficulty, the awful elusiveness of Atlantis
and the perils of the quest, might be illustrated by a
satirical novel. An appropriate title would be *From Boots
to Bats* and in it there would be a central character, Aunt
Jane, whose search for Atlantis, the Unattainable, is the
theme of the book. To be readable such a novel would
require to be written in the lightest vein, very human,
very farcical but never cruel; for the object of the book
would be to serve as a grim warning to all who become
"interested" in the famous Isle. Let us sketch a possible
plot, based upon a few facts about Atlantis.

A chance conversation with a fellow Rotarian in Sidcup
causes Aunt Jane to go to the local Boots' Circulating
Library in search of a book about Atlantis. The young
lady in charge has only Dennis Wheatley's *They Found
Atlantis*, but undertakes to enquire if there is any further
literature upon the subject. Aunt Jane, a serious old lady,
scorns Dennis Wheatley's admirable novel because it is
too light, and after a wait of several weeks, during which

her appetite for the truth is greatly whetted, the library notifies her to the effect that there are 1700 works on the subject; but since most of them are either out of print or in foreign languages, and since they (Boots) suppose that Aunt Jane can't in any case manage them all, they herewith enclose a list of the five latest to choose from. Aunt Jane, according to the terms of her "on demand" subscription, selects two . . .

This is the beginning of a strange obsession which within the space of a few months transforms a sweet mild old lady into the Terror of Sidcup Rotary circles.

Even the vicar is relieved when, a year later, two men wearing white coats come to take her away. Aunt Jane cannot understand why these men are so kind and gentle with her. They actually seem sympathetic when she tells them that she is Lotus, the incarnation of the spirit of the last Queen of Atlantis. (At this point the story is nearer tragedy than comedy and the reader, who has already been assured that Aunt Jane has no hereditary insanity in her family and no trace of Latin blood, can fully appreciate the reasons for her mania ; in fact he has become so sympathetic towards Aunt Jane that the end of the book leaves him uncertain whether she was not really Lotus after all and far saner than the doctors who took her to the asylum.)

But what is the inner history of this unfortunate obsession?

Aunt Jane, the type of all maiden ladies who are susceptible to crazes, begins by convincing herself emotionally that Atlantis was a continent in the Atlantic ocean which was engulfed 10,000 years ago in a terrible cataclysm. The idea inspires her with a comfortable nostalgia, for she dislikes the racket of 20th century life. Reasonably however—Aunt Jane is also a tenacious rationalist—she finds that it is not so easy to believe this. Modern books tell her that Atlantis is a question which must be approached scientifically; and this view seems to her to be very sensible. Unfortunately she cannot properly distinguish between the scientists who deal in facts, and the "scientists" who merely rationalize their speculations. She soon discovers that the "scientists" approach the subject from different angles, and that they contradict each other with such freedom that nearly every book seems to refute some other book. Undaunted by this and believing with almost superstitious reverence in the high disinterested motives of all scientists, she plunges into the melée of treatises and tracts and dissertations to which she is entitled by the terms of her "on demand" subscription at Boots, with only the dimmest understanding of the questions at issue. It is not enough for her to read a little archaeology. She must also bother her head about geology, ethnology, biology, philology, comparative theology, and suboceanic-physiography. Studies upon Atlantis have been written from the viewpoint of all these branches of knowledge and poor Aunt Jane has not the means of judging which are really important and which are irrelevant. She finds that some are technical and very dry, whereas others make such

17

B

startling and dramatic claims that even she—innocent and trusting—is a little suspicious of their value and wonders if their authors are real scientists. They set out to prove that Atlantis was not situated in the Atlantic Ocean, but in Lybia, Crete, Palestine, Spitzbergen, the Sahara, Nigeria, Mecklenburgh, Upsala, Ceylon, and America—to mention only a few of the suggested sites. There are authors who, not content to look for Atlantis alone, maintain that it was merely another name for Lemuria, the Pacific continent, or Mu, the Motherland of Man. Aunt Jane is convinced by them all in turn; but it puzzles her sadly that they fail to convince each other. This makes her reflect a good deal about human nature and the meaning of knowledge. Even worse is the fact that many of the best books are in foreign tongues and have not been translated into English; she knows no German, Spanish, or Norwegian and has only a smattering of French, with the result that she frequently has the feeling that she is missing something of vital importance.

The more learning she acquires, the more certain she becomes that her studies are lamentably incomplete, that she is further than ever from the solution of the problem. To start with, she possesses none of the instincts of a bluestocking. Her brain reels with its burden of unwonted and largely useless information, and her reason, still goaded by her indomitable will, begins to give way. She neglects her parish work. Worse still, her preoccupation with Atlantis has already cost her many of the faithful and sympathetic friends who nursed her through previous bouts of Seventh Day Adventism and Plymouth Brotherhood. Her doctor warns her that her health is deteriorating and advises her strongly to give it up. But she persists gamely, thrusting aside all friendly advice.

At the blackest period Aunt Jane finds the Light. Atlantis has been explained by the Occultists. Here at last is Peace, Unanimity and Science. She becomes a Knower, an Illuminate, proud in the knowledge of a secret tradition which has never died since the black day when the Atlantic waters closed over the island. Before she saw through a glass, darkly. But now, face to face. It is perhaps a little unreal, but exciting and mysterious. And so Aunt Jane inherits the wandering spirit of Lotus.

She is quite happy when the men come to take her away to a large house right in the country . . .

But this novel must remain unwritten. The plot is perhaps after all too slight to be worthy of Atlantis or Aunt Jane, and the book might offend where no offence was intended.

It has been authoritatively stated[1] that Atlantis is a "problem" which is "mainly geological." This is true, in so far as Atlantis is nothing more than a problem. But it should be added that for many people the solution of this geological problem and the assent to it of the learned world is a matter of secondary importance. There will always be people for whom Atlantis has an essentially romantic appeal and for them the uncertainty of its position on the borders of fact and fable gives it a distinctive quality that would be lost directly the learned pronounced it to be the "dawn of history" or the "cradle of culture." And since it may as well be admitted that the balance of responsible scientific opinion is against Atlantis ever having existed at all, though a fuller case can now be stated for it than has hitherto been possible, there is an obvious need for a new approach to the whole subject. Now that a scientific impasse has been reached, it looks as if the interest must temporarily shift, pending further discoveries which will enable the scientists to arrive at an absolute concensus of opinion, from the extremely technical problem "Did Plato's Atlantis really exist, and if so when and where?" to the more general question: "What is the *value* of Atlantis?" This general consideration resolves into a number of minor questions, all more or less new, which suggest a more fruitful approach for some years to come.

(*a*) How far does Atlantean literature reflect human nature and the development of thought at different stages in the history of the legend?

(*b*) Why has the story always appealed so strongly to the occult imagination?

(*c*) What is the secret of the vitality and stamina which has given the legend a longer life than any great traditional story that has come down to the modern world?

With the emphasis on the value of Atlantis the definition

becomes easier, and the inconclusive scraps of scientific evidence which are so eagerly snapped up and with such difficulty digested by those whose only concern is to put Plato's island on the map of history, begin to assume their proper proportion. So also do the attacks of the sceptics who consider belief in the existence of a real Atlantis to be a sign of lunacy.

But the sceptics cannot be completely confounded, for the amount of energy and reputation that has been wasted in dragging red Atlantean herrings across the trail of the public is paralleled only in the annals of Baconism; and the folly is not confined within the covers of books.

In 1926 the Société d'Etudes Atlantéenes was founded in France. In the next year a schismatic section of the society broke off and founded a new society with a review called *Atlantis*. The rivalry between the groups grew so strong that finally, during a meeting at the Sorbonne at which the Société d'Etudes Atlantéenes was discussing the history of ancient Corsica, the proceedings were violently interrupted when two tear-gas bombs were thrown into the hall by some rival Atlantomaniacs, euphemistically described in the report of the proceedings as "visionaries." The object of this "group of dreamers" which objected so demonstratively to the scientific methods of their rivals, was apparently to go for long hikes wearing Atlantean emblems in their buttonholes. They had Atlantean picnics and the initiates spoke a strange jargon derived from the technical vocabularies of Cabbalists, Freemasons, Boy Scouts and Celtic Bards.[2]

Introduction

As a further example of the lengths to which people may be driven by the desire to put Atlantis on the map, the activities of a group of Danish scientists deserves an honourable mention. In 1933 this group organised and founded the Principality of Atlantis. Their leader, Prince Christian of Denmark, a direct descendant of Lief Ericsen, who "discovered" America centuries before Columbus, has been given the title of "Prince of Atlantis." The society (reputed to have already a membership of over 25,000) exists for the purpose of elucidating the mystery by study and exploration. Its members are confident that they will establish not only that Atlantis existed as a continent, but also that it still exists under the sea. The measure of their assurance may be gauged by the fact that they have already issued stamps and money and even designed a flag for the Principality of Atlantis.[3]

A curious gem of Atlantean aberration is the famous Schliemann document. In 1912 Doctor Paul Schliemann, a grandson of Henry Schliemann, the great German archaeologist who discovered the sites of ancient Troy and Mycenae, published in the *New York American* an article called *How I discovered Atlantis, the source of all civilisation*. In this article the author declared that among some secret papers left by his grandfather at his death were certain documents concerning Atlantis. He also stated that his grandfather, upon his death-bed, scribbled a note charging whoever opened the secret papers to break the "the owl-headed vase." On the outside of the envelope containing the papers was a further note to the effect that it was not to be opened except by a member of the archæologist's family who would pledge himself to devote his life to research on the lines indicated by the contents of the envelope.

Paul Schliemann then described how he took the pledge and set to work on his grandfather's notes. He began by breaking the vase with the owl's head. In it was a square of silver-like metal with the inscription in ancient Phoenician characters: *Issued in the Temple of Transparent Walls*. In another envelope the elder Schliemann said that when making his Trojan investigations he had found among the treasures discovered in the second city a peculiar bronze vase of great size: "within it were several pieces of pottery, various small images of some peculiar metal, coins of the same metal and objects made of fossilized bone. Some of these objects and the bronze vase were engraved with a sentence in Phoenician hieroglyphics *From the King Cronos of Atlantis*.

"You can imagine my excitement," said Doctor Schliemann; "here was the first material evidence of that great continent whose legend has lived for ages . . . This material I kept secret as the basis of investigations which I felt would prove of infinitely more importance than the discovery of a hundred Troys."

The result of Paul Schliemann's researches was to establish a chain of evidence proving without any doubt the existence of Atlantis. The proofs were based upon the close correspondence of the ancient civilizations of the old and new worlds which could only be accounted for by postulating the existence of a common original in the Atlantic. This correspondence he established by comparing a very satisfying collection of prehistoric objects, some of which his grandfather had discovered and some of which came to light through his own efforts. He also deciphered an ancient Maya text in the British Museum (MS. Troano) and found that it contained the same story as a Chaldean MS. which came from a Buddhist temple in Lhasa. Both told a tale of cataclysm concerning a country called Mu.

"What can be the significance of these two accounts, one of Tibet and the other of Central America, which tell of similar cataclysms and both refer to a country called Mu?

"But if I desired to say everything I know, there would be no more mystery about it." So ends the article in the *New York American*.

There were a number of further proofs which Paul Schliemann promised to elaborate in a forthcoming book.

But his claims were so sensational that suspicion was at once aroused in archæological circles, and a number of German critics declared that the whole story was bogus. And this, indeed, seems to have been the case. In the first place no one has yet succeeded in deciphering the Maya script and Schliemann's account of the destruction of Mu seems to be directly derived from Dr Augustus le Plongeon's *Queen Móo and the Egyptian Sphinx*, in which the author claimed to have read a number of Mayan inscriptions, including MS. Troano, and to have solved the mystery of Atlantis.[4] Secondly the book promised by Paul Schliemann never appeared, and the author himself remained silent on the subject. The Chaldean MS. and the owl-headed vase never came to light, nor did any of the other objects mentioned in the article. Close examination of Schliemann's line of research showed that he had been very much influenced by Ignatius Donelly's *Atlantis, the Antediluvian World*, which had had a great success in 1882. But perhaps the most conclusive evidence against Paul Schliemann was the testimony[5] of his grandfather's collaborator, William Dörpfeld, that to the best of his knowledge Henry Schliemann never made any deep study of the Atlantis question, and, although he had heard him speak of it on several occasions, he did not believe that he left any original work on the subject. Alexander Bessmertny makes this comment on the Schliemann mystery: "It is clear that the anxiety to prove the existence of Atlantis combined with a desire to make a reputation as a scientist prompted an excitable person, tired of bearing an illustrious name, to resort to doubtful means to make the question even more obscure by an essay in mystification."

Perhaps the oddest of all freaks in Atlantean literature is *Atlantis: die Urheimat der Arier*, published in 1922, by Karl Georg Zschaetzsch. According to Zschaetzsch the Atlanteans, or blònde blue-eyed Aryans, lived since the beginning of things in a state of high moral civilization. But the southern part of Atlantis was suddenly annihilated by a hail of fireballs from the sky, caused by a comet. Only three Aryans survived: Wotan, and his sister and daughter. The daughter was born during the fiery deluge and from her sprang the whole human race. Unfortunately the descendants of these original Aryans intermarried with non-Aryans on the mainland and created a mixed and decadent strain. In the pure Aryan days the race had been vegetarian, but after the deluge the vitiation of the race caused the mixed descendants of Wotan to become carnivorous. Another sign of racial decadence was the introduction of intoxicating liquor by a girl called Heid, a non-Aryan witch who practised the loathly science of preparing fermented drinks, the source of infinite evil. (Such, according to Zschaetzsch, is the proper interpretation of Eve giving the apple to Adam). Gradually the Atlanteans spread West. The Greeks were Atlantean colonists and Zeus merely an important Greek-Atlantean chief.

Then comes the unsuspected dénouement. It turns out that the whole point of the book is to show that the author is descended from Jupiter. Zschaetzsch is merely a corruption of the name Zeus! One wonders if the Third Reich has been able to exploit the talents of Karl Georg Zschaetzsch.

This kind of absurdity, which is by no means uncommon in Atlantean literature, has been so canvassed that it is not hard to see why unsympathetic critics of the pseudo-

Introduction

scientific search for Atlantis have got the notion that everybody who is interested in the subject must be tainted with lunacy or charlatanism. In his edition of Plato's *Timaeus* and *Critias* Professor Taylor remarks, apropos of some of the wilder efforts to "place" Atlantis that: "fancies of this kind have long disappeared from serious history and ethnology, though they still seem to have a curious fascination for the imperfectly educated." There is a good deal of truth in this, for "perfectly " educated persons are seldom given to strong enthusiasms outside the sphere of exact sciences. But the fact is that "education" in the academic sense has little to do with the degree of sanity or insanity with which people speculate about Atlantis; what is necessary is not a public school education or a B.A. Oxon. but a sound liberal education on Erewhonian lines, crowned if possible by what Samuel Butler calls "a degree in Hypothetics at the Colleges of Unreason." Most of the writers about Atlantis have lacked this extra qualification. They have studied things rather than people, and by approaching scientific matters in an emotional state they have invited the sneers of sceptics. Many have been learned enough. Among them there have been professionals turned amateur, specialists lured from the particular to the general, and practitioners become idealists. And the reason for the frequent oddity of their conclusions is that they have failed to realise the relation of Atlantis to human nature, its subtle correspondence with their own subjective character, their religious, nationalistic or "escape" desires.

27

They lose themselves in the study and become absorbed to the point of oblivion; a state which is bliss, but fatal to preserving a balanced judgment in a highly controversial matter. They begin to believe only what they want to believe and interpret the available evidence accordingly. If the evidence is insufficient they try to increase its importance by false emphasis, sophistries, evasions and unauthenticated assertions; and often the faking is so well done that the general reader, lacking special scientific knowledge, falls an easy prey to specious reasoning. Intuition plays an important part in the various attempts to present a rational case for Atlantis, and later we shall see how this affects the scientific problem.

Another characteristic of the literature in favour of the Atlantean hypothesis which tends to damn it academically is the way the books are written. In tone they are generally either excessively assertive or else excessively humble. Both are protective and are intended to ward off the inevitable criticisms which experience has taught Atlantophils to expect. The desire to put Atlantis on the map bears much the same relation to serious archæology as the Oxford group does to the Church of England; it fosters a sectarian spirit, paralysing to adequate self-criticism. That is why writers who try to approach Atlantis from an individual angle tend to fly to the opposite extreme and become unreadably dry.

But the universally readable book from this point of view will probably not be written for many years. To write it at the present stage of stalemate would require something more than wide scientific knowledge. It would require something of the inspired guesswork of Columbus, something of the insolence and swagger of the picaroon who pursues his way through Don Quixote and the works of Smollett no less arduously for being a figure of fun, and also, not least, a certain reverence for the labours of others in the past, however discredited they may be by contemporary standards of "scientific" Atlantean study. Thus the little tragedy of the main body of Atlantean literature is that it falls between two stools. On the one hand the scholars interested in the subject have not the necessary range of imaginative perception; and on the other the amateurs have not the power of marshalling the facts and drawing the right conclusions from them—a power which ensures that the works of more erudite persons shall at least meet with respect, if not with enthusiasm. In this way it happens that the best writers about Atlantis are often hostile to the theory that it actually existed. While denying the reality of Atlantis they are better able to appreciate the poetical and philosophical truth of the story than the Atlantomaniacs, Atlantophils and Atlantologists whose desire to be scientific makes them shun the seductive qualities of the legend like the plague.

The bibliography of Atlantis, as compiled in 1926 by Jean Gattefossé and Claude Roux, mentions some 1700 items. In the last ten years that list must have been greatly extended. Then why another book?

The first justification is the lack of English books on the subject. The second is that the majority of these 1700 are either out of date or not worth reading for one or other of the reasons mentioned above, most of the books written before the middle of the 19th century can be deliberately omitted, since they propound hypotheses or admit as scientific, opinions which have been invalidated by scientific progress. Thirdly one may plead the permanent interest of the subject itself. It does not matter that the real existence of Atlantis is highly questionable; nor that science has little to add for the present to the controversy; for the fact remains that at various periods of the world's history Atlantis has existed in the minds of civilized people and in their maps, too. The legend is like a coloured thread running right through the existing fragment of man's pattern; it is a living tradition and will continue to be handed down until another deluge wipes the record of its existence from the archives of the human race. It follows then that if people are bored with Atlantis it is the fault of those who take it upon themselves to transmit and elaborate the story. Like life itself it must go on being restated in the effort to improve on previous attempts.

THE STORY OF ATLANTIS

What shall we tell you? Tales, marvellous tales
Of ships and stars and isles where good men rest,
Where nevermore the rose of sunset pales,
And winds and shadows fall towards the West:
JAMES ELROY FLECKER.

(1)

It has been written that a good and glorious race once
flourished in Hellas, 11,400 years ago. It sprang from the
soil in that part of the world which came under the divine
government of Pallas Athene and Hephaestus. At the time
of the sharing out of territory among the gods Pallas had
chosen Hellas for herself, because she perceived that the
well-tempered climate was ideal for the evolution of a virile
and intelligent people. All turned out as the goddess had
planned. She was a shepherdess who guided her people by
persuasion rather than by force and the result was a
civilization which was peaceful in the knowledge of military
strength and contented in the wisdom of its social order.

Both the country and the civilization were very different
from the Attica of classical times. The country was extremely
fertile and the Attican peninsula, which in historical times
became like the skeleton of a body wasted by disease, was
formerly covered with exceedingly rich soil, unmatched
by any other soil in the world for the variety and quality

of the harvests it produced. The mountains were abundantly forested with fine timber and there were no bare rocks and crags betraying the framework of the land through the rich soft soil. The fertility of the land was maintained by its ability to store up the rains; and whereas in later days the precious rain ran away down the bare mountain sides to lose itself in the sea, the soil then contained lower strata of non-porous potter's clay which stored up the water so that it percolated into the hollows and irrigated the whole land with plentiful springs and rivers.

The people living on this land of plenty were true husbandmen. They throve in the midst of natural plenty and loved all that was noble. They put their best into the soil and the soil gave them full measure in return. But it was in the city that the true character of this civilization was most evident. Life was simple and not too luxurious. Houses were neither splendid nor mean and they used the finest materials for private and public buildings compatible with their unostentatious and communal way of living. But they made no use of gold or silver for building or for any other purpose.

An important feature of this civilization was specialization in all walks of life. The priesthood was strictly separated from the other classes. The urban craftsmen plied their own trades independently, and so did the hunters, farmers and herdsmen. Also separated and depending entirely upon the other citizens for their means of livelihood were 20,000 soldiers of both sexes, the guardians of the city. They were forbidden by law to follow any other calling but that of war, and lived apart in a great compound surrounding the temple of Athena and Hephaestus upon the side of the acropolis. The acropolis in those days was much larger than the one known to the later day Greeks; that was because of a deluge which washed all the soil away in one night, and left only the bare hill.

Many stories of the valour and goodness of this people were known to the prehistoric world, but one in particular surpasses all the others in heroic splendour. Ancient Egyptian records told of another great power in those days, a proud people who lived on an island in the Atlantic ocean beyond the Pillars of Hercules (the name given by the ancient world to the Straits of Gibraltar). At that time the Pillars of Hercules were navigable, but a few centuries later the straits were silted up so that ships could no longer pass out to the open Atlantic.

The name of the island was Atlantis. It was larger than North Africa and Asia Minor put together and from it seafarers could make their way to other islands and thence to the opposite continent which, according to ancient belief, encircled the whole of the ocean. In this island a great and marvellous monarchy had arisen, and a capital city far grander and more spectacular than that of Athens. Its kings boasted descent from the gods, an origin even more glorious than that of the Hellenes whom Athene caused to spring from the earth. At that time, when the gods were

C

dividing the earth into lots so that they could establish their temples and sacrifices among mortals, the island of Atlantis fell to Poseidon.

Near the sea in the middle of the longest part of the island there was a fertile and beautiful plain. Fifty furlongs from the centre of this plain was a hill where lived three aboriginal mortals, a man named Evenor, his wife Leucippe and their daughter Clito. Just at the time when Clito had reached maturity her parents died and Poseidon, falling in love with her, took her as his wife. To secure his love, he enclosed the hill with alternate rings of sea and land, so that no man could get to the island in the middle. Counting from the centre there were two rings of earth and three of sea at equal distances from one another. The central island he enriched with all natural advantages. At his command two fountains flowed from underground springs, one hot the other cold, and the soil began to produce food-plants of every kind. When he had finished his work—an easy task for a god—he begat five pairs of male twins and dividing the island into parts, allotted one part to each. The eldest of the first-born pair received the best of the inheritance, the island which was his mother's home and the land surrounding it. He was called Atlas, and after him the ocean was called Atlantic and the island Atlantis. His twin, whose name in the language of his country was Gadirus, in Greek Eumulus, received the part of Atlantis facing Gadira (Cadiz and the surrounding country of the Gadirantes.) All the other brothers received portions of Atlantis and the adjacent islands, and they and their successors ruled over them as subject princes. But the kingship was vested in Atlas, from whom sprang a prolific line of kings, the throne descending always to the eldest son for many generations.

By exploiting the natural resources of the empire these kings in time amassed great wealth, but it was the island itself which produced the main necessities of life. Stone and metals were excavated in considerable quantities from the earth including one metal which was the most valuable of all metals except gold. This was orichalc, known to the classical world more as a name than a reality; but the Atlanteans made great use of it, for it was so brilliant that it glowed like fire. There were forests whose mighty trees provided timber for building houses and shelter for numerous wild animals, including elephants, which roamed wild among them. There was every kind of vegetable food necessary for supporting life, besides a great abundance of aromatic plants and delicious fruits to charm the voluptuary by their variety and quality.

The general physical character of the island was mountainous. The mountains were very high and beautiful, with lakes, rivers and meadows, and in them lived a thriving population. They surrounded the plain upon which the city was built upon three sides, coming right to the sea-coast. The plain, which faced South and was sheltered by a screen of mountains on the North side, was level and smooth. It measured 3,000 furlongs in one direction and at the centre stretched inland 2,000 furlongs from the coast; naturally almost rectangular in shape, generations of Atlanteans had achieved the almost incredible task of making it mathematically rectangular by carrying a fosse right round it, 10,000 furlongs long, a furlong broad and 100 feet deep. Into it flowed the water courses from the mountains on the land side of the plain and circulating the plain it met the city at a point on the south side and was carried out to sea by the main canal. Parallel with the east and west sides of the fosse straight canals, 100 feet wide, connected the mountain-side with the seaboard at regular intervals of 200 furlongs; they were joined by oblique channels of cross communication. These canals were used for conveying timber and produce from the mountains to the city. In the summer, when there was a shortage of rain, they were also used for irrigation purposes by the farmers, who were thus able to secure two harvests annually.

The three rings of land round the original home of Poseidon and Clito were bridged over so that people could pass over to the palace built in the central island. They began by cutting a canal from the sea to the outermost ring of water, 50 furlongs long, 300 feet broad and 100 feet deep. The largest vessels could sail right into it and dock there. At the bridges over the rings of water they made openings in the land big enough to admit a single trireme. The rings of land were considerably above water level and the openings in them were roofed over so that ships passed through from one ring of water to another by a

subterranean passage. The outer ring of water, to which the
sea canal had been made, was 3½ furlongs wide and so was
the contiguous ring of land. As for the second pair of rings,
the water and land were both 2 furlongs broad. The ring
of land surrounding the central islet was 1 furlong broad.
The island where the palace stood was 5 furlongs in
diameter. The whole centre, land and water, was enclosed
by stone walls, and towers and bridges were built over the
bridges where the sea flowed in. The stone, which was
black, white and red, the Atlanteans quarried from beneath
the central islet and the inner ring, thus making extra
basins for shipping which had the advantage of being roofed
with the natural rock. Sometimes they built their houses
of a single coloured stone and sometimes the colours were
mixed so as to give a variegated effect. The outside of the
surrounding wall was covered with a coat of copper, the
inside with tin, and the walls of the actual acropolis with
orichalc which glowed like fire.

Within the acropolis was the palace, which had been
built by the first kings and beautified by each succeeding
monarch until it became a marvel of size and splendour.
In the very centre, fenced off by a golden railing was an
untrodden sanctuary sacred to Poseidon and Clito, the
birthplace of the Atlantean race. Nearby was Poseidon's
own temple, a well proportioned building but very splendid
and quite different from a Greek temple, for the whole
of the exterior was coated with silver except for the figures
on the pediments, which were of gold. Inside, the roof

was of ivory, ornamented with gold, silver and orichalc. Walls, columns and pavements were also covered with orichalc. The temple contained gold statues of Poseidon standing in a chariot drawn by six winged horses, so large that his head touched the roof; round him were golden statues of a hundred Nereids riding upon dolphins. There were also many statues dedicated by private persons. Outside the temple were statues of all who had been of the number of the ten kings, and their wives. In the citadel, hot and cold springs of great medicinal value flowed into a system of covered and open basins for the public use. The waste water was conducted to the grove of Poseidon where it helped the excellent soil to produce a magnificent and varied collection of trees, and was then led into the outer rings of water by means of conduits at the bridges. On the rings there were numerous temples to different gods, as well as gardens and gymnasia. On the outer ring of land there was a racecourse running round the whole circumference. Barracks had been erected on both sides of the racecourse for the main body of the state guardians; some of the more trustworthy men were billetted in the inner ring nearer the citadel, and in the citadel itself was the king's bodyguard, consisting of the pick of the military.

The dockyards of the inner ring of water were filled with triremes and their equipment. At a distance of nearly 50 furlongs from the outer ring of water, a wall, starting from the mouth of the canal connecting with the sea, encircled the whole city, returning to the other side of the canal mouth. It was filled with a multitude of densely packed houses and the large harbour and canal was constantly busy with merchant vessels arriving and departing. Day and night passengers were embarking and disembarking and the walls rang with the incessant clamour and shouting.

The whole countryside was divided up into allotments, 60,000 in number, each having an area of 10 square furlongs. The owner of each allotment was bound to furnish the sixth part of a war chariot, two horses, an attendant and a charioteer, a light chariot without a seat, two hoplites, two archers, two slingers, two stone-throwers, three javelin men and four sailors, to make up the full complement of 1,200 vessels.

Each of the kings was absolute in his own territory, but their relations with one another were regulated by the commands of Poseidon as laid down by a law of the earliest kings inscribed upon a column of orichalc in the sanctuary of Poseidon. On the column, besides the laws, was written an oath calling down curses on the disobedient. The kings assembled in this sanctuary at alternate intervals of five and six years, to do equal honour to the even and the odd numbers.

During these sessions they debated about common affairs and, if anyone had broken the law, he was judged by his peers. When they were about to give judgment they first of all exchanged pledges. This was done in the following manner. In the sanctuary consecrated bulls roamed wild. Hither the ten kings came unattended and each prayed to Poseidon that he might capture the bull preferred by him. Then they chased the bull with wooden clubs and with cords; no other implements were used. As soon as they had captured one of the bulls they brought it to the column and cut its throat over the orichalc, the blood flowing down the inscription. Having sacrificed the bull, it was burned as an offering, and some of its blood was mingled in a bowl of wine, each king casting in a clot. The rest was thrown into the fire. They then drew the wine from the bowl in golden beakers, make a libation over the fire and swore to give judgment according to the Laws. When each had taken the pledge for himself and his house after him, he drank and dedicated his beaker to the sanctuary. Afterwards they all repaired to a banquet.

At dead of night when the sacrificial fires burnt low, they returned, dressed in deep blue robes, and sitting round on the bare earth, proceeded to extinguish the embers. The business of judging and being judged then began. When dawn came they recorded their judgments on a plate of gold and dedicated it with their ceremonial robes as a memorial.

This federation of Atlantean states had many special laws governing the rights of kings, but there were three chief ones. The kings were pledged not to bear arms against one another; and if any king attacked the royal house of another city, the others automatically came to the rescue of the attacked city. They were to take counsel with one another in case of war or any other national emergency; and in event of common action being taken the house of Atlas was acknowledged as the leader. But this suzerain had no power over the lives of his kinsmen save with the approval of the majority of the ten.

For many generations the Atlanteans obeyed these laws out of devotion to their ancestor Poseidon. They were good, humble and judicious. They counted their prosperity a little thing, perceiving that they could only maintain their spiritual wealth by restraining their lust for the material gain which came to them so easily through the abundance of their natural resources. But as the divine strain of Poseidon became increasingly faint through successive generations marrying with humans, the mortal temper began to predominate and their ideas changed. They became greedy for even more wealth and power than they already had; and their fortune became their downfall. They grew imperialistic and acquisitive in national as well as in private life.

Zeus perceived the decadence of the Atlanteans and determined that they should be judged. He gathered together all the gods and held a great council to decide the best way of bringing them to book.

At that time the Atlantean empire extended on the African side from the straits right to Egypt and in Europe as far as Tyrrhenia. But not content with an already large empire, the Atlanteans attempted to enlarge their boundaries to include Egypt and Greece and their allies on the shores of the Mediterranean. But Greece showed herself equal to the struggle, and now at last the excellence of her civilization was manifest to the whole world. When all her allies had been enslaved till she alone was still free to defend her liberty, she made a supreme effort and, drawing upon all her resources of heroism and energy, she managed to overthrow the invaders. Then she liberated all the peoples who had been enslaved by the Atlanteans and set herself up as the protector of all those countries threatened with subjugation.

But the war never reached a natural conclusion. Fate intervened in the form of a series of terrible earthquakes and floods. In one dreadful night and day the entire Greek army was swallowed up by the earth. Atlantis also sank into the sea and vanished for ever, taking with it its warriors, its temples and grottoes, and the whole elaborate and beautiful city which the Atlanteans had evolved through the centuries. The only trace of its existence was to be found in the great shoals of deep mud which made impassable for ships those parts of the Atlantic where the island had sunk.

(2)

That is the substance of the story which is found in the Platonic dialogues *Timaeus* and *Critias*. Both purport to be records of actual conversations between Socrates, Timaeus, Hermocrites and Critias which took place in the house of

The Story of Atlantis

Critias in Athens supposedly about 421 B.C., when Socrates was under 50 and Plato still a small child. Of the *dramatis personæ* the only character who need concern us is Critias, since it is he who tells the story of Atlantis. He is evidently intended to be Plato's own great-grandfather and a very old man, over 85. The setting of the *Timaeus* and *Critias*, as in other Platonic dialogues, is historical, in the sense that they recreate the personalities and conditions of the generation before Plato. Probably these dialogues were intended by their dramatic form to reach a wider public than the purely learned audiences who gathered to hear Plato lecture at the academy.

The *Timaeus* opens with references to a discourse delivered " yesterday " by Socrates, which is shown by a summary of its contents to be the *Republic*. Actually Plato wrote the *Timaeus* many years after the *Republic*—the first five books of it at any rate—and the idea of linking it with his earlier work must have been an afterthought, since there is nothing in the *Republic* to suggest that he was contemplating a continuation at the time of composition. But the relation of the *Critias* to the *Timaeus* is that of a direct sequel, though again there is good reason to believe that some years separated the dates of composition of the two dialogues.[1] The *Timaeus* announces the story of Atlantis, and also anticipates it by a brief summary of the events in the war between the prehistoric Athenians and the Atlanteans which is later to be fully described in the *Critias*.

In the *Timaeus* the story of Atlantis is introduced by

43

Critias. He tells it to please Socrates who wants to hear an heroic tale illustrating the soundness of the ideal state, the workings of which he has just recalled for the benefit of the company.

"Here then, Socrates, is the story; extraordinary as it is, it is absolutely true, as Solon, the wisest of the wise Seven, once declared. Solon, who, you must know, was as he says in several places in his poems, a kinsman and friend of my great-grandfather Dropides, told my grandfather Critias (so Critias, in his turn, used to repeat the story to me in his old age), that there are great and splendid ancient exploits of our city which have been forgotten from lapse of time and decay of population, and, in particular, one, the greatest of all. To commemorate the exploit to-day would be a becoming way at once of showing our gratitude to you, and honouring our goddess on her festival, with a true and loyal hymn of praise."

Socrates: "Well said, indeed. But pray, of what nature was this authentic, though unrecorded, ancient exploit of our city of Athens, as described by Critias on the faith of Solon's statement?"

Critias: "I will tell you, though it is a long while since I heard the story, and the narrator himself was far from a young man. In fact, Critias was, at the time, by his own account, on the verge of ninety, and I myself some ten years old. We were keeping the Apaturia, and the day was the Curiotis. Well, we boys celebrated the festival in the regular customary way; our fathers set us to recite verses

against one another for a prize. Of course various com-
positions of different poets were repeated, and, in particular,
a good many of us boys sang Solon's verses, which were
novelties at the time. So one of the confraternity observed
—it may have been his real opinion, or he may only have
meant a compliment to Critias—that Solon had been, in
his judgment, not only one of the wisest of men, but, in
his verse, the most free-spoken of all poets. The old man—
how well I recall the scene!—broke into a delightful smile.
'Ah, Amynander,' he replied, 'if he had given himself to
verse seriously, like others, and not made a mere pastime
of it; if he had completed his treatment of the story he
brought home from Egypt but was forced to lay aside by
the faction-feuds and other disorders which he found here
on his return; then in my judgment, no poet's reputation—
not that of Hesiod or Homer—would have stood higher
than his.' ' And what story was that?' says the other. 'That
of a mighty achievement, worthy of superlative renown,
once accomplished by our city, though, owing to lapse of
time and the destruction of those who accomplished it,
the tale of it has not lasted down to our age.' 'Let us
have the whole,' says the other. ' What was the story
Solon related as true? How did he come to hear it and
on whose testimony did he tell it?' 'In the Egyptian delta,'
said Critias, 'where the Nile splits into its several mouths,
there is a region called the Saitic nome, of which the
principal city is Sais, the native place, as you know, of
King Amasis. The goddess who presides over this city is

called Neith in the Egyptian language; in Greek, as the inhabitants say, her name is Athene; the citizens profess to be warmly attached to Athens and, in some sense, connections of ours. Well, Solon said he visited this city and was received there with great honours. In especial, he made enquiries about ancient times from such priests as were most conversant with them, and so discovered that neither he nor any other Greek knew anything to boast of about such matters. Once, being minded to lead them into talk about antiquities, he began to tell them the most venerable of our legends, those of Phoroneus, the reputed first man, and Niobe; then he went on to tell the story of Deucalion and Pyrrha, how they fared after the deluge, to trace the pedigrees of their descendants, and to try to compute the years which had elapsed since these events by a reckoning of the times. 'Ah Solon, Solon,'says one of the priests, an exceedingly old man, 'you Greeks are always children; there is no Greek that is a greybeard.' 'How do you mean that ?' says Solon when he caught the remark. 'You have all boys' minds,' says the priest, 'ancient tradition has stored them with no venerable belief nor any hoary lore. And the cause is this. Many and divers are the destructions of mankind which have been and shall yet be; the greatest are wrought by fire and water, but there are others, slighter, wrought by countless causes. Thus the report which is current even among yourselves that Phaeton the Sun-child once harnessed his father's car, but being unable to guide it in his father's track, scorched the face of the earth and

46

was himself consumed by the thunderbolt, has indeed the semblance of a mere fable, but the fact of it is a deviation of the bodies which revolve in heaven about the earth and a destruction, coming at long intervals, of things on the earth in much fire. Hence, at such times, those who dwell among mountains and in highlands and high places perish more completely than dwellers by rivers and the sea. As for us the Nile our universal preserver, then preserves us from this peril also by his rising. On the other side, when the gods cleanse the earth with a flood of waters, while the herdsmen and shepherds in the mountains come safe off, dwellers in your cities are swept by the rivers into the sea. But in this land of ours, neither then nor at other times does water descend on the fields from above; its way is ever to ascend from beneath. These are the causes and reasons for which the traditions preserved here are reputed the most ancient of any, though in true fact, in all regions where excessive rains or heats do not forbid it, there are always men to be found, sometimes more, sometimes fewer. And whatever has come to pass that is heroic or grand or in any way memorable, in your own land, or here in Egypt, or in any other region that has come to our ears, the records of all this have from old times been written down here, in our temples, and are kept safe; whereas, with you and the rest of mankind, life has but just been furnished with the art of writing and the other requisites of cities, when the torrents come down on you from heaven again, at the usual period, like a pestilence, and leave behind them only the rude and the unlettered. Thus you revert, so to say, to your childhood and know nothing at all that has befallen in ancient times, in our country or in your own. Why, Solon, the story you have just related of past generations in your own land is not much better than a tale of the nursery. Your people can recall but one deluge though there were many before it, and, what is more, you do not know that the bravest and noblest men of all history once existed in your own land. You and all your fellow citizens are sprung from a scanty remnant of them, though you never suspect this, because their survivors for many generations passed away without utterance in writing. Yes, Solon, once on a time before the great Deluge, what is now Athens was a city right valiant in war and with laws in all things exceedingly excellent. Her exploits and her polities are said to have been the noblest of all under heaven whereof any report has come to our ears.' When Solon heard this, he was amazed and besought the priest with much earnestness to tell him the full tale of those our citizens of old in order. So the priest made answer: 'Solon, I will not stint you, the tale shall be told for love of you and your city, but, chiefly, of the goddess, your patron, foster-mother and tutoress and ours. Yours she was first, taking over the seed of you from Earth and Hephaestus, ours later by a 1,000 years. Now the age of our native institutions is recorded in our sacred writings as 8,000 years. So I will unfold to you in a few words the laws of your citizens of 9,000 years ago, and the noblest of their exploits;

the full and precise story shall be related some other time, at our leisure, with the very texts before us. First then, compare your laws with ours here in Sais; you will still find among us many an illustration of those you then had.'"

Critias then sketches the civilization of ancient Attica, as the priest told it to Solon, his great grandfather's friend. The war with Atlantis is summarized, with this conclusion: "Afterwards came a time of extraordinary earthquakes and inundations. In one terrible night and day of storm, your warriors were swallowed in a body by the earth, and Atlantis likewise sank into the sea and vanished. This is why the Ocean in this part to this day cannot be navigated or explored, owing to the great depth of the mud caused by the subsiding of the island.

"This, Socrates," Critias continues, "is a succinct account of the story told by old Critias, as he had heard it from Solon. It all came back to my mind yesterday, as you were discoursing of your state and its citizens, and I was surprised to observe your wonderful and significant coincidence on so many points with Solon's narrative. Still I preferred to say nothing of it at the moment; after so many years my memories were imperfect. I resolved then that I would not repeat the story until I had first gone thoroughly over the whole in my own mind. That was why I was so ready yesterday to fall in with your injunctions; in a case like this, I said to myself, the great thing is to propound a theme which meets the wish of the company, and we shall not have much difficulty about that. So, as Hermocrates

D

has told you, I began at once to communicate my reminiscences to our friends on my way back home yesterday,
and when I had got home, I spent the night in making a
pretty complete review of them. How true the saying is
that we have a wonderful memory for what we learn in
childhood! I hardly know whether I can recollect all I heard
yesterday, but I should be much surprised if I have lost
a single detail of this story, though it is so very long since it
was told me. You see, it gave me a great deal of sport and
enjoyment to listen, and the old man was delighted to
answer my repeated questions; thus it has all been impressed
on me like the lines of an indelible design. In fact, I told it
all exactly to our friends early this morning, that they might
be provided with a subject as well as myself. So here I am,
Socrates—this is the point I have been so long in coming
to—ready to tell the story not in outline, but with full
details, as I heard it myself. We will translate the citizens
and the city of which you were discoursing yesterday from
fiction to fact; the city we will take to be our own Athens,
and the citizens of your imagination we will identify with
those actual ancestors of ours of whom the Egyptian priest
talked. I am sure they will fit the part, and we shall not
strike a false note if we say that they are the very Athenians
of that distant time."

The rest of the dialogue is taken up with a discourse on
cosmology and natural science delivered by Timaeus.
Critias does not continue his account of Atlantis until the
later dialogue. Plato's evident object in splitting it up is to

encourage the reader who is bored by Timaeus's talk on science with the promise of something to come with a "human interest" about it.[2] There is also literary artistry in foreshadowing the account of the splendour of Atlantis with the knowledge of its fate. Otherwise the Atlantean story has no logical connection with the "matter" of the *Timaeus*.

Both dialogues are the works of Plato's old age and it seems certain that the *Critias* was written some years later than the *Timaeus*. The *Timaeus*, though a difficult text, shows signs of careful revision for publication. But the *Critias* is evidently no more than a rough draft left unfinished at Plato's death and published afterwards without editorial supervision. This is the conclusion drawn from the extreme grammatical difficulty of the text, the sketchiness of the account of the Atlantean civilization compared with the detailed account promised by Critias, and the fact that the dialogue breaks off suddenly at the crucial point in the story. As Plutarch says in his life of Solon: "the only thing that Plato ever left imperfect was the Atlantic isle." Scholars explain this in various ways. Plato may have found his interest flagging and turned from the *Critias* to devote the last years of his life to writing the *Laws*; or old age may have so impaired his mind that he was incapable of finishing it; or again he may have intended to finish it and died before he was able to. But all these explanations seem to ignore one point; the significance of the precise moment at which the story told in the *Critias* breaks off.

Critias is describing the decadence of the Atlanteans, how the "God's part in them began to wax faint by crossing with much mortality . . ." "To the seeing eye," he says, "they now began to seem foul, for they were losing the fairest bloom from their most precious treasure, but to such as could not see the true happy life, to appear at least fair and blest indeed, now that they were taking the infection of wicked covet and pride of power. Zeus the god of gods, who governs his kingdom by law, having the eye by which such things are seen, beheld their goodly house in its grievous plight and was minded to lay a judgment on them, that the discipline might bring them back to tune. So he gathered all the gods in his most honourable residence even that which stands at the world's centre and overlooks all that has part in becoming, and when he gathered them there, he said . . ."

Surely a strange place to break off, just when he is about to explain the whole moral dénouement of the story? The break is so sudden and unexpected that at a first reading it suggests a parallel with Coleridge's unfinished poem, *Kubla Khan*. For the "person from Porlock" who so inopportunely interrupted Coleridge we might substitute a "person from the Piraeus" calling to pay his respects to the great academician or perhaps bringing news of Dion from Syracuse. But a closer examination shows the break to be a logical one, in the sense that the writer of a tragedy, or, better, an epic might naturally put down his pen and pause to think before beginning on the climax; also, of course, we have no reason for supposing that even if Plato had been interrupted he could not have continued afterwards. And yet, knowing that he did not continue the work, there does after all seem to be something involuntary about that discontinuance. If we momentarily exclude the possible intervention of death or paralysis it seems a little improbable that senility or boredom would have prevented him from trying to finish a work which was not only far advanced but also the completing link in the chain: *Republic, Timaeus, Critias*. But there is another explanation. Is it not possible that Plato was still in full possession of his faculties and anxious as ever to leave no loose ends, yet *unable* to go on because he realized that he had reached an impasse?

The question at once arises, what is the real theme of the *Critias*? According to Professor Taylor "the moral of the story is to be that a morally sound public and private life will secure a nation against the greatest superiority in numbers and technical equipment on the part of the adversary." But if that is the *moral* to be drawn from the result of the war between the Atlanteans and the prehistoric Atticans, it is also clear that the *theme* of the fable may be taken to concern the relations of the gods and human beings. Zeus is the agent of divine retribution for the wickedness of the Atlanteans who have departed from the simple way of life and have become luxurious and imperialistic. We know from the *Timaeus* what was to be the result of the council of the gods and it is reasonable to suppose that in the unfinished speech of Zeus, Plato was to have asserted:

Lost Atlantis

Eternal Providence
And justified the ways of God to men.

How Plato intended to reconcile the purpose of Zeus with
the final annihilation of the Atlanteans, or what part, if any,
Poseidon would have played in determining their fate,
we cannot guess. Perhaps Plato did not know himself.
But the point is that the theme of the fable, as it stands, is
one of divine retribution; and in his treatment of it Plato
anticipates Milton's treatment of the Fall theme in *Paradise
Lost*. He sets out to reconcile man's misfortunes with the
benevolent purpose of the gods; and the result of the
attempt is a dramatic success but a moral failure. The dice
is loaded against the Atlanteans from the first, for the
"god's part" in them is bound to "wax faint by admixture
with much mortality." Without freewill in the matter of the
race, their decadence is inevitable, and the judgment of
Zeus therefore incomprehensible in human terms. Hence
the city of Atlantis and its inhabitants recall the sufferers of
Aeschylean tragedy sacrificed to the jealousy of gods; and
like Satan and the rebel angels in *Paradise Lost* they arouse
the reader's sympathy. Zeus becomes the instrument of a
cruel fate. The prehistoric Greeks, whose civilization is
intended to be the ideal of simple goodness and classic
restraint, seem frankly dull, whereas the lavish and luxurious Atlantean civilization, which reflects perhaps in its
architecture and its wealth of precious metals Plato's conception of the gorgeous and licentious East, transcends all
questions of "taste" by its strong appeal to the imagination

and the senses The fact that the Athenian army also perishes at the destruction of Atlantis merely confuses the issue. The Athenians are permitted to vindicate the sound moral of their civilization only for a "little hour," and then they meet the same fate as their decadent opponents. This apparent inconsistency is difficult to explain, unless we suppose that Plato drowned his Greeks for purely practical purposes, to account for the lack of a later historical tradition about the Atlantean war in his own country and to make the story of the Egyptian priest seem more probable: this, on the whole, seems to be the best explanation.

But in any case the fate of the Greeks is not interesting; Atlantis and its citizens are the "heroes" of the drama and the reader's sympathies are with them from the beginning. Warned in the *Timaeus* that Atlantis is doomed to destruction, there is tragic irony in the description of the material splendour and vast scale of the city, its wealth of colour and movement, its elaborate political organization. For the city itself is even more important than its inhabitants, and when it is overwhelmed by the sea, the tragedy lies in the uniqueness of the marvel that is lost to the world. Its like will not be seen again. It is submerged irrevocably and with it the living symbol of an ideal which, if barbarian, is at least grand. It is, in a sense, *too* grand. One feels that Plato was so carried away from his original intention by the poetry of the theme, that the fable got beyond his control. He started as a philosopher and then found that despite himself he had become one of those dramatic poets whom,

55

in the 3rd book[3] of the *Republic*, he accused of under-
mining the prestige of the gods. One passage in the *Republic*
seems particularly relevant. "Then let us not believe, once
more, or allow it to be said . . . that any other god-sprung
hero could have ventured to perpetrate such dreadful
impieties as at the present day are falsely ascribed to them;
rather let us oblige our poets to admit, either that the deeds
in question were not their deeds, or else that they were not
the children of gods; but let them beware of combining the
two assertions, and of attempting to make our young
believe that the gods are parents of evil . . ." This surely
is precisely the error that he himself has committed in the
Critias. His Puritan purpose became submerged, as did
Milton's in *Paradise Lost*, and he found himself forced
either to abandon it altogether or to continue in a position
so illogical that it would have been a negation of his whole
philosophy. In particular, it had been one of his most
inflexible principles that all wrong-doing was involuntary,
that no one can know the good and do the bad. This had
always seemed to him an essentially practical principle,
an incentive to educate people to determine what the good
was. But in the *Timaeus* and *Critias* we see the same
principle turned into a tragic theme, the futility of human
efforts to be rational in a world which is ordered by the
incomprehensible logic of the gods. We may guess that
while he was writing the *Timaeus* and *Critias* Plato felt
rather than perceived the tragedy of Atlantis and that it
was not until he reached the dénouement that he realized

quite how inconsistent the work had become and decided to abandon it. To account adequately for the apparent emotionalism in the treatment of the theme is of course impossible; too little is known about Plato's life. But the failure of his teaching in Sicily may have had something to do with it. He could scarcely help feeling a certain responsibility for the increasing muddle of Sicilian politics, which he had tried so hard to disentangle in his long association with Dionysius II and Dion. He had often said that the "good" man is the man who is efficient and successful, and it must have been bitter to have had to recognize that he himself had achieved so little of practical value outside the academy.

From the probable relationship of Plato's late works to the circumstances of his life it seems logical to infer that when he stopped short of the judgment of Zeus in the *Critias*, he then turned to redeem the remaining years of his life in writing, or at any rate in continuing to write, the *Laws*. Both fall within the last twelve years of his life, 360–348 B.C. and their exact chronological relationship cannot be determined, but the fact that the *Laws* provide the completest possible contrast with the *Critias* suggests that he did not actually begin to write them, even if he had them planned, until after he had finished with the *Critias*. The *Laws* is a completely practical work, evidently based upon Plato's own experience in Syracuse, and intended to serve as a model of legislature for the new cities that were beginning, at the end of his life, to spring up in place of the old democratic city-states. The practical nature of the *Laws* suggests very much the "making good" of a philosopher whose contention had always been that philosophy had to be useful to be worth while; and both in this and in the studied avoidance of any dramatic element, he seems to have turned his back on the *Critias*.

So the *Critias* remains a mere fragment, and probably repugnant to its author; a philosopher's failure and therefore of little importance among Plato's works. But it is also possible to see in it the raw material of a poetic achievement which might have stood high among the masterpieces of literature. Or, if Plato had been able to resolve the tempestuous personal discord which the fable seems to symbolize—the sense—intellect antithesis—we might have had an imaginative work similar to the *Tempest*,[4] embodying the fundamental oppositions of Plato's nature and resolving them, like Prospero's, to the rich and strange music of a happy old age. But Plato could not prevent the Atlantic tempest from overwhelming Atlantis, either because he felt bound to accept the integrity of a story derived from ancient tradition, or perhaps because there was no music in his soul and therefore he could not, with Prospero, renounce his high philosopher's calling and say:

> when I have requir'd
> Some heavenly music—which e'en now I do—
> . . . . I'll break my staff,
> Bury it certain fathoms in the earth,
> And deeper than did ever plummet sound
> I'll drown my book.

For Plato perhaps there would have been something tame
about the epilogue

> And my ending is despair
> Unless it be relieved by prayer.

That way out would have seemed too easy for one who
had been accustomed all his life to mental fight.

The fact that the Atlantean story emerges as a great
myth from the troubled fragment of the *Critias* is therefore
in a sense *despite* Plato, an important point when we come
to consider its relationship to later history.

(3)

Where did Plato get the story of Atlantis? Did he invent
it, or was he really working, as he makes Critias say, upon
a genuine tradition? The question is vitally important,
since Plato's account is not only the earliest but the sole
documentary evidence of the existence of Atlantis. The
name does not appear connected with any island in classical
literature before Plato, and his account is the basis of all
that has been written about the subject for over 2000 years.
For this reason many of the best writers on Atlantis have
thought it necessary to try and establish the historical
truth of the letter of the story told in the *Timaeus* and the
Critias, and their efforts to prove their case have led them
into a fundamentalism which is demonstrably mistaken.
Plato's story, whatever it is, is certainly not history. But it
also is probable that it is not entirely fable. There is reason

59

for believing that it is a mixture of the two, a traditional story representing a mass of irrelevant or imaginary material gathered round a small core of historical fact. Separating the core from the accretions can only be done by guesswork and inference, but once it is admitted that there is sufficient evidence for believing in the possible existence of an Atlantic isle independently of Plato, then the method of dissecting the Platonic dialogues becomes justified. The history of the legend of Atlantis must be studied as a whole, like a strange tree that can be identified not only by digging round the roots but also by sampling the berries that grow upon the topmost branches and by watching the birds which perch upon them; from the behaviour of these birds it is possible to tell quite a lot about the tree. From the colour and shape of bark, berries and leaves, one can learn still more. Its reaction to storms is a test of strength and shows how deep the roots go into the ground.

If we see the problem of Atlantis in this way, it is obviously less disillusioning than some of the more pious Atlantophils have imagined, to find that Plato "invented" parts of the story; for there remains the comforting possibility that even if he deliberately fabricated the whole thing, he might have hit upon the truth by mistake and anticipated mythologically what was later to be described scientifically.[5] But many people now think that such a theme as Atlantis cannot be "invented." It is too universal and important to be evolved in the consciousness of one man independently of some traditional memory.

In examining Plato "as to credit," the first thing to notice about the *Timaeus* and *Critias* is the careful documentation which has often been used as evidence for the authenticity of the whole story. The account of the descent of the legend from Solon to Critias, Plato's own great grandfather, and of the existence of manuscripts in Plato's family is so well done as to be almost convincing; but it should nevertheless be clear that Plato is using a very common literary device.[6] As Professor Taylor has pointed out, the pretended documentation anticipates the "old manuscript" which is so dear to the romance writers from Horace Walpole down to Fenimore Cooper and Jules Verne. Pierre Benoit's *L'Atlantide*, the story of the finding of Atlantis in the Sahara, which is supposed to be contained in a manuscript confided by a young Spahi lieutenant to his sergeant, is an obvious modern example of the literary fake. The fake in Plato's case should be apparent from the fact that the "papers of Solon," which are represented as family heirlooms, have never been heard of by anybody outside the family. Also there is a suspicious contradiction in his account of his transmission of the Solon story. In *Critias* (vi 13b) Critias says: "His actual papers were once in my father's hands, and are in my own to this day." But elsewhere (*Tim.* vi, ii 3b) he tells his audience that he has been reflecting all night to try and remember the story he heard in his youth, and before beginning it he invokes the muse of memory (*Crit.*1 8d). "She is the power on whom the whole fortune of my

discourse most depends." Now why, if he had the MS., did
he have to rely on his memory? And further, if he were
really relying on memories of a story heard in his youth,
could he, even with the assistance of the Muse, recall the
story in such extraordinary detail, giving the exact measurements of canals and buildings? In the *Timaeus*, Critias
significantly declares that "the great thing is to propound
a theme which meets with the wishes of the company, and
we shall not have much difficulty about that." T. H. Martin,
however, who is hostile to the Atlantean theory, thinks that
Solon may well have heard the story from the Egyptian
priests, but that they invented it in order to flatter the vanity
of the Athenians and to secure their alliance. Yet on the
strength of the objections mentioned above this seems
scarcely likely. If the story really did come from Egypt, it
is surely more probable that Plato himself heard it when
travelling in the country, as he very probably did. At any
rate it looks as though the family tradition must be rejected.

Another suspiciously literary touch occurs in the *Critias*.
"Before I begin my narrative," says Critias, "I must make
a brief explanation, or you may be surprised to hear of so
many barbarians with Hellenic names. So I will give you a
reason for this. Solon had a fancy to turn the tale (of
Atlantis) to account in his own poetry; so he asked questions
about the significance of the names and discovered that the
original Egyptian authors of the narrative had translated
them into their own speech. In his turn, as he learned the
sense of the name, he translated it back again, in his manuscript, into our own language . . . So if you hear names

like those of our own countrymen, you must not be surprised . . . ". Such attention to detail seems too studied to be really convincing. As for Solon's poetic activities, in particular his projected epic, there is no external evidence to corroborate the family tradition about it, though Plutarch, in his life of Solon, says that Plato was "ambitious to cultivate and adorn the subject of the Atlantic island as a delightful spot in some fair field unoccupied, to which also he had some claim by his being related to Solon . . ." by which Plutarch means, surely, that Plato accepted Solon's connection with a traditional story of Atlantis which also happened to suit him particularly well because of his descent from the great man. Doubtless Plato by embellishing and enlarging upon the story intended to pay a tribute to Solon's memory, whether the connection was real or not. But in general Plato's attention to realism and dramatic probability suggests a fake more than a purely fabulous treatment would have done. The Greeks did not properly discriminate between history and myth, and if Plato had not been pretty sure that his story of Atlantis would not be taken seriously he would scarcely have bothered to make it so real. From the contemporary standpoint it would have seemed too historical to be history!

Without examining the legend too closely, then, there is some reason to suspect the literary fake. We know, too, that Plato occasionally illustrated his dialogues with moral stories, such as the tale of Er the Armenian in the last book of the *Republic*. And these doubts are not dispelled by the history of the legend after Plato. For 300 years after Plato's death there is no direct extant commentary upon the story. That is curious, even allowing for the possibility that relevant texts may have been lost. For the first direct information we have to descend to Strabo the geographer (B.C. 54) who tells us that Poseidonius, a 1st century Stoic, believed the story of Atlantis to be true; but Strabo himself mocks his excessive credulity. Pliny the Elder, a credulous man, is also sceptical. But Proclus says that Crantor, a Platonist of the first academy, admitted the perfect truth of the story. He cited in his support the testimony of certain priests in Egypt who showed to contemporary Greeks some columns upon which the story was written. Proclus also speaks of a certain geographer called Marcellus (1st century B.C.) who says in his *Ethiopics* that the traditions of Atlantis were collected by travellers to a remote island. Proclus further states that the question was hotly debated in the academy at Alexandria, which was the centre for intellectuals in the 1st and 2nd centuries. He himself, his master Syrianus and several other Neo-Platonists all believed it to be true history.

But opinions are very divided, outside as well as within the academy, and it is impossible to draw any definite conclusion from them. The full history of opinion on the subject is to be found, fully catalogued, in T. H. Martin's famous edition of the *Timaeus* (*Études sur le Timée de Platon*. Bk I). From the diversity of these opinions Martin concluded that a historical basis for the story was improbable, but he qualified this by adding that the diversity is partly due to the amateurishness and lack of learning of the various writers. "Many scholars," he wrote, "setting sail in quest of Atlantis with a more or less heavy cargo of erudition, but without any compass except their imagination and caprice, have voyaged at random. And where have they landed? In fifty different places."

But apart from the academic controversy centring round the authenticity of Plato's story, there are certain passages in ancient literature which have often been quoted as referring to Atlantis, though they do not actually mention it by name. The most famous of these passages is in the *Historical Library* of Diodorus, the Sicilian historian who lived in the time of Caesar. It describes (see appendix C) a great island situated far out in the ocean west of Libya. The island is fertile and mountainous, the mountains heavily wooded, the climate temperate with numerous gardens watered by soft springs and producing abundant fruits. The description is certainly reminiscent of parts of the *Critias*, but Diodorus speaks of the island as though it existed in his own day. Elsewhere (see appendix C) he refers to some people called Atlantes, inhabiting a rich fertile country to the north-west of Libya near the ocean and far more civilized than the surrounding tribes. The Atlantes claimed that their country was the cradle of the gods and that their first king was Uranus. There were many cities throughout the country; and the capital was called Cerne. But in those days there also lived in western Libya a tribe of warlike women, the Amazons, ruled by a queen named Myrina. "A longing having come over them to invade many parts of the inhabited world," these Amazons marched into the country of the Atlantes and sacked Cerne with such thoroughness that when the inhabitants of the other Atlantean towns heard of the disaster that had overtaken their capital they all surrendered to Queen Myrina; but those who capitulated were treated honourably and Myrina built a new city over the ruins of Cerne, permitting the captives and any other natives who so desired to settle there. The new city bore her name and, taking the Atlanteans under her protection, Myrina waged a successful war on their behalf against a hostile neighbouring tribe, the Gorgons, afterwards retiring to her own borders.

But here again it is difficult to see any reference to Atlantis. The city of Cerne is not on an island and Diodorus himself tells us that the Atlanteans got their name from Atlas.

Another writer who perhaps tells us about Atlantis is Theopompus of Chios, a Greek historian of the 4th century B.C., whose work survives only in the *Various Histories* of Aelian. He reports a conversation which took place between Midas, King of Phrygia, and Silenus, a demi-god, in which Silenus tells him that the known world consists of three islands, Europe, Asia and Libya, all completely surrounded by sea; outside, there is nothing but a huge continent with many big cities and a great abundance of gold and silver. One of these cities was extremely warlike and its warriors determined to penetrate into our islands. After crossing the ocean with 2,000,000 men they reached the country of the Hyperboreans. But they thought them contemptible people and did not deign to pass into the regions beyond. (See Appendix C).

The value of this testimony is that it is contemporary with Plato's; and therefore, if we believe the writer and acknowledge the points of resemblance between his account and the Platonic dialogues, it may be cited as evidence for a common tradition. Aelian himself, however, does not believe Theopompus to be a trustworthy author.

The fact that Atlantis slept beneath the ocean for 300 years after Plato told of its sinking has done a lot to encourage the sceptics in their belief that he fabricated the story. But it is often forgotten that this neglect was probably largely due to Aristotle's widely canvassed view that Atlantis was a myth. A much more serious snag is the absence of any mention of Atlantis by writers *before* Plato, especially Herodotus, who had visited Egypt; for if there was a current tradition there it is surprising that it should have escaped him. Herodotus does, in fact, mention the *Atlantes*, but they are described as inhabitants of Lybia, living in a tall hill like a tower, which is known to the natives as the Pillar of Heaven. They are also vegetarians and have no dreams. It is difficult to believe that they have any connection with Plato's Atlanteans, though those who believe that Atlantis itself was situated in Libya naturally contend that they have. But Herodotus does not like committing himself to statements unsupported by what he considers to be good testimony. He says that he cannot speak authoritatively about the extremities towards the west. In another passage he states that he has been unable to get any eye-witness account of a sea on the other side of Europe although he has taken great pains to find out. As to the Egyptian tradition, Professor Glover[7] repeats Mr Llewelyn Griffith's opinion that Herodotus when travelling in Egypt (100 years after Solon), was probably just as dependent upon guides for what he heard and saw as any modern tourist visiting a foreign country for the first time; and that he probably missed a great deal more valuable information than would be possible now that there is a standard of what is interesting to the tourist. In any case, he himself expresses contempt for the stories told him by the priests of Sais, which suggests that he may very well have heard something rather like Plato's story but chose to disbelieve it for lack of proof.

(4)

With Homer there is more to go on. Though he does not actually mention the name Atlantis, it is quite possible that Scheria, the island of the Phaeacians in the *Odyssey*, is connected with Plato's island. The question has been hotly debated, but the identification of Scheria and Atlantis is now treated with more respect than when Ignatius Donelly first suggested it in his *Antediluvian World*.

Donelly wrote: "The wanderings of Ulysses, as detailed in the *Odyssey* of Homer, are strangely connected with the Atlantic ocean. The island of the Phaeacians was apparently in mid-ocean:

> we dwell apart, afar
> Within the unmeasured deep, amid its waves
> The most remote of men; no other race
> Has commerce with us;

The description of the Phaeacian walls, harbours, cities, palaces, ships, etc., seems like a recollection of Atlantis. The island of Calypso appears also to have been in the Atlantic ocean, 20 days sail from the Phaeacian isles; and when Ulysses goes to the land of Pluto, the 'underworld,' the home of the dead, he

> reaches the far confines of Oceanus

beyond the pillars of Hercules. It would be curious to enquire how far the poems of Homer are Atlantean in their relations and inspiration. Ulysses' wanderings were a prolonged struggle with Poseidon, the founder and god of Atlantis."

The resemblance between Plato's Atlantis and the city of Alcinous is certainly very striking. Odysseus was astonished by the "long lofty walls of the city with palisades atop." He lingered spellbound before the palace, not daring to cross its "golden threshold." The palace ceilings shone like the sun and moon. Its walls were covered with copper. The gates were gold with silver lintels, silver posts and gold door-handles. The great banqueting hall was lit by the flare of torches held in the hands of golden

youths. Outside the palace was a marvellous garden.[8] Two
streams flowed through it, one turned into ducts irrigating
the whole garden, the other carried underground to the
palace, where the townspeople could draw water from it.
The Phaeacians were the best sailors in the world; but
when they sailed Odysseus safely back to Ithaca, they
aroused the wrath of Poseidon, who had already done his
best to drown him on the voyage from Calypso's island and
would have succeeded but for the timely intervention of
Athene. Alcinous realized that Poseidon had his knife
into the Phaeacians because the Phaeacian ship which
was returning to Scheria after taking Odysseus back to
Ithaca was smitten "into a rock of her own size and shape
quite close to the shore." He therefore proposed to sacrifice
twelve bulls to Poseidon "that he may have mercy on us
and not overshadow our city with a high mountain," as
Nausithoos, the father of Alcinous, had prophesied.

The resemblances are curious, and in particular the last
part suggests that Homer was working on a tradition of
some volcanic island such as there is reason to believe that
Atlantis, if it existed, must have been. But in spite of the
resemblances, the differences are marked enough to exclude
the possibility of a direct relation between the *Critias* and
the *Odyssey*. It is more likely that both contain elements of
the same tradition, or elements of different versions of the
same tradition.

The best approach to the problem of the relation of Plato
to Homer is that suggested by Walter Leaf in his *Homer*

and History. "Scheria has its place in the map of poetry and fancy; and there I believe it can be identified. Is it not Homer's name for Plato's Atlantis? And if we want some connection with the real world, let us think of the ingenious and attractive idea which finds in Atlantis a recollection of the Minoan Empire, and consider whether the Phaeacians, who, in Nausicaa's words, 'care not for bow and arrow but only for masts and oars and ships' may not fairly remind us of the men of Knossos, who, secure in their rule of the sea, never cared to fortify their palace by the shore." So far, so good. But, first, what is this theory which finds in Atlantis a recollection of Minoan Crete?

The last great period of Cretan history, 1700–1400 B.C., is known as the Late Middle Minoan or Palace Period. At that time Knossos, after at least two cycles of depression and recovery followed by even greater prosperity, had achieved its grandest civilization. There is no parallel in the ancient world for the splendours of Knossos: for the vast palace of Minos, apparently haphazard in the labyrinthine layout of its winding passages and courtyards and sanctuaries, yet beautiful in the detail and colour of the delicate frescoes and statuettes which give us glimpses of a society so sophisticated in manner and dress that we are reminded of the French Court at Versailles. Unique, too, is the elaborate system of drainage, superior to any system in use even in the Middle Ages; and the curious organization of life by which the Palace was not the exclusive residence of the monarch, but a sort of capital city containing the Exchequer,

the Arsenal and the Government Offices as well as a
sports ground and bull-ring for the amusement of the
populace. The Palace also included the granaries and
store-houses, the oil-vats and oil-presses which not only
represented the sovereign's personal wealth but were also
the main economic and industrial centre of the whole
community. There is no doubt that this palace system was
as highly organized in its policy as it was "modern" in its
luxury and refinement. As an important indication that it
was a high type of civilization we have the archaeological
evidence that the cities were not even fortified, but the
island relied, like Britain, upon a powerful and efficient
navy to protect its shores.

The Cretan Empire was a federation, consisting of
scattered island cities under the control of the central
government at Knossos. It was the dominant naval and
commercial power in the eastern Mediterranean and its
influence was widespread, extending north-west over the
sea-coast of the Greek peninsula and south to Egypt, Inner
Palestine and the Middle Orontes. At all times Crete traded
with Egypt and throughout the history of the two powers
their fortunes seem to have been closely linked; but during
the Palace period the contact was not so close as it became
later in the Mycenaean period.

About 1400, when Crete was at the peak of its power and
prosperity, disaster came. With dramatic suddenness, the
palace of Minos and many other Cretan cities were
destroyed, in circumstances which have provided one of

the greatest mysteries of prehistory. There is evidence that fire, devastation and pillage came upon the city unawares. The whole elaborate and palatial structure of Knossos crumbled, as it were, overnight, never to be reconstructed.

Until recently Knossos was thought to have been raided and sacked by a foreign invader at a time when the Cretan Fleet was at sea, leaving the shores of Crete unguarded. The catastrophe was believed to have been due to the successful rebellion of Cretan colonists of the Greek peninsula, who seized a long-awaited opportunity to free themselves from the yoke of Knossos. Some held that the invader was Theseus, reported in legend to have been born and bred by the sea and to have established himself at Athens as heir to the throne; in which case he might well have been a Cretan colonial, a Mycenaean. That would fit in very well with the theory of a rebellion against the central government of Knossos,[9] due perhaps, as the Cretan legend suggests, to a custom by which a yearly tribute was levied upon the mainland dependencies of Knossos.[10] But Sir Arthur Evans[11] has now pronounced his final verdict, that the destruction of Knossos was due to an earthquake, a recurrence of the terrible seismic disturbances which had already caused havoc at least twice in Cretan history. This earthquake was followed by widespread fires and it is probable that the populace took advantage of the confusion to pillage the houses of the nobility.

That was the end of Knossos and though civilization of a sort continued in Crete the splendours of the palace of

73

Minos were not renewed. Instead, the catastrophe of Knossos marks the beginning of the rise of Mycenae as an important mainland power inheriting many of the features of the palace empire. This Minoan-Mycenaean empire flourished only till about 1300 B.C. when it, in turn, became absorbed by another, "Achaean" civilization. Who exactly the "Achaeans" were remains unsettled; but it is probable[12] that they were a feudally organized confederation of peoples from Greece, Rhodes, Crete and Asia Minor, dominated by the princes of the Homeric "House of Atreus" with headquarters at Mycenae and Sparta. This Achaean period of Minoan history was also shortlived. By 1000 B.C. the ancestors of the classical Greeks, the Dorians, had invaded the peninsula and the last shreds of Minoan civilization and the splendid traditions of Knossos and ancient Mycenae were obliterated from the "Greek" consciousness. As the priest of Sais remarks to Solon in the Timaeus, the oldest Greek greybeards were childishly ignorant of the past history of their country.

One feature of the Mycenaean-Minoan civilization which succeeded the old Palace empire of Knossos was a more intimate relationship with Egypt. From 1400–1300 B.C. Mycenaean traders were familiar figures in the Egyptian ports. But with the rise of the Achaeans as the new type of Cretan this relationship became strained by the aggressive behaviour of the federation. An Egyptian chronicler recorded, somewhat ominously, that "the islands were troubled in the midst of the sea." Egypt became alarmed by the policy of the federation and in 1280 B.C. Ramases II made an alliance with his old enemies, the Hittites, which was a pact of mutual assistance against the increasing attacks of the "Peoples of the Sea." In the reign of his successor Ramases III, the storm broke. Egypt was invaded by a confederate host which seems to have included Achaeans, Danaans, Philistines and Libyans. But Ramases was equal to them and in a great battle he shattered the confederation on sea and land, and delivered Egypt from the menace.

This was in 1190 B.C. About this time came the Trojan war as a result probably of the break-up of the defeated federation, and despite the success of the Achaeans their return to Greece marks the beginning of the decline which culminated in the Dorian invasion.

In February 1909 an anonymous letter appeared in *The Times* pointing to the extraordinary parallel between the "facts" of Cretan history (as shown in the light of current archaeology) and the story contained in the *Critias* and *Timaeus;* also to the resemblance between the palace of Minos at Knossos and the citadel of Atlantis, as described by Plato. The author of the letter, the late K. T. Frost, later developed his theory more fully.[13] In Crete, he said we have a historical case of a mighty island civilization, similar to Atlantis both in its political organization and the general appearance of the city of Knossos, suddenly and dramatically destroyed by an "Athenian" invader, and as

75

a consequence the Minoan empire collapsed. Moreover, the "Athenians" enjoyed only a short-lived triumph. Soon after their victory they themselves fell a prey to invaders from the North (the Achaeans). From the Greek point of view this sequence of events might conceivably have become condensed by later tradition into a story of a great Athenian victory immediately followed by a disaster similar to the one which, according to Plato, destroyed both the Atlanteans and their Athenian foes at the same time. A tradition of cataclysm, Frost claimed, could be produced by the fact that later-day Greeks, inheriting tales about the Crete of the palmy Palace period, would fail to associate them with the drab Crete of their own day, and would therefore conclude that the Palace Crete was a different island altogether which had disappeared before their time. Some such tradition might have survived to influence Plato. As an illustration of the process we have Homer's account of Scheria,[14] the island of the Phaeacians in the *Odyssey*, which was "substantially true of the great period of the palace of Knossos, but quite unlike Crete as he knew it."[15]

According to K. T. Frost a similar process took place in Egypt. The fall of Knossos did not mean the end of Minoan civilization, but only the "palace" form of it. We can illustrate the point from the relations of England and America in the 18th century A.D. which are roughly analogous to those of Crete and her mainland colonies up to 1400 B.C. Suppose that the cities of England, during the American War of Independence, had been destroyed in a great earthquake; our civilization would not have perished. On the contrary the Anglo-Saxon race and language, besides a great many English traditions and customs, would have been preserved in the U.S.A.; to a contemporary foreigner American civilization might have seemed to be a mere transplantation of British. Similarly, Cretan civilization, far from perishing in the catastrophe of 1400 B.C., actually became more widespread under Mycenae, though of a lower type. But the Egyptians could not distinguish properly between the Minoan and Mycenaean periods; for one thing the Mycenaeans probably looked and dressed much the same as the earlier Minoans with whom they had been accustomed to trade and no doubt many of them spoke the same language. When, therefore, in the later Achaean phase, these Mycenaean Cretans appeared among the sea-raiders who were defeated by Ramases III in 1190 B.C. it is possible that the Egyptian chroniclers recorded the battle as the end of Minoan civilization, thus laying the traditional foundation for Plato's account of the islanders who conquered all North Africa as far as Egypt and perished in the attempt to invade it. From the Egyptian point of view at any rate, the story of Cretan civilization was complete.

That the Egyptians were in the habit of accurately recording Cretan history as far as it concerned them is proved by the survival to this day of inscriptions describing the invasion of the sea raiders. But Frost pointed out that their records of events which did not directly concern them were very much vaguer, and that after the attempted invasion caused Egypt to sever all relationship with the "Cretans," they confused this part of Minoan history with earlier records relating to the fall of Knossos. They had already perhaps recorded somewhat vaguely the sack of the great island empire of Knossos by raiders led by an "Athenian," and there must have been plenty of stories current to preserve the memories of the palace civilization. Add to all this the attempt at universal conquest and condense the whole, and we have the principal ingredients of the story of Atlantis. "The main outlines of the story told by the Priest about Atlantis contain a true account of the closing scenes of Minoan history from an Egyptian point of view; there was a great island empire in the far west; it did make an attempt at what seemed to the Egyptians universal conquest; the islanders were defeated by raiders from Greece who were very possibly led by the chief lord of Athens; and these "Athenians" were not long afterwards in turn overwhelmed.

"Thus both Greeks and Egyptians had records of the old Minoan civilization before the sack of Knossos. Both of them came in time to know Crete well, but neither connected the island with that particular civilization, though the Greeks knew that Minos had once ruled there with fabulous wealth and magnificence. This unidentified civilization must therefore have once belonged to a land that had since disappeared with its people. They were

78

already familiar with a flood tradition. What more natural than that this ancient and unknown people had also been overwhelmed in a flood? In this case, the transposition of the island and the theory of the flood, and indeed the whole Atlantis legend in its popular form, is due to lack of identification."[16]

Now the first part of this theory can no longer be considered as valid. As we have seen, Knossos was destroyed by an earthquake. There was no "Athenian" invasion of Crete, and Sir Arthur Evans even considers it likely[17] that the régime of the priest-kings of Knossos, far from ending with the destruction of the palace, was actually transferred to a mainland site, probably to Mycenae itself, at this time "redecorated according to the latest Knossian fashion." In any case the Achaean "conquest" of the Mycenaeans is thought by many to have been a slow rise to power by peaceful penetration. Hence, the "facts" of Cretan history can scarcely now be regarded as an adequate basis for a subsequent tradition about a great Athenian victory over an island people, followed by disaster to the conquerors. It is fairly evident that Plato did not get the story of Atlantis from the detritus of Greek records of Cretan history, even if such a tradition could have survived the avalanche of the Dorian invasion.

With Homer's story we cannot be so sure. Assuming the historicity of the Scheria episode in the Odyssey[18]—as we have to for the purpose of argument—the Phaeacian

79

seamen and athletes and dancers, and the sumptuous palace of Alcinous are altogether foreign to the Greece of the Achaean or heroic period in which Homer probably lived. On the other hand the decoration and general scheme of Phaeacian life is quite consonant with the earlier Mycenaean period on the peninsula as revealed by the excavations at Mycenae and Tiryns, and Homer could easily have inherited descriptions of it without reference to any specifically Knossian tradition.[19] Yet we are still left with the fact that Scheria is an island;[20] and here the rival claims of Minoan Crete and Mycenaean Corfu as Homer's original have to be considered, though neither satisfactorily fills the bill.

The essentially Minoan features of Scheria are the palace architecture; the fondness of the Phaeacians for music, song and dance; the emancipation of the Phaeacian women; and certain manners and customs. On the other hand some aspects of Scheria are definitely non-Minoan. These are: the fortified walls of the city; the lack of any mention of bull-fighting, the chief sport in Minoan Crete; and the fact that Nausicaa says "amongst us Phaeacians the bow and quiver get no honour." The Cretan bowmen were famous. Another, almost insuperable objection to Crete as Scheria is the unlikelihood that perhaps only 300 years after the destruction of Knossos, an educated Achaean who could read the records and was probably well travelled should so far forget the position of Minoan Crete as to place it in the remote west, where Scheria is evidently intended to be. Odysseus actually mentions Crete and Minos during the course of his story in the hall of the Phaeacian King Alcinous.

Corfu conforms much better to Nausicaa's description of the Phaeacian people as the "ultimate race of men." Ancient tradition identified Scheria with Corfu,[21] and as Professor Shewan has pointed out[22] it would be the final port of call for the Minoan traders on the voyage west; also its pleasant and fertile countryside would correspond with what Homer tells us of Scheria. But though a temple has been found which shows Mycenaean influence, no Mycenaean remains have actually been found there; so that if we are to equate Scheria and Corfu the process implies rather a large assumption. Another difficulty crops up when we begin to look for Homer's authority for Poseidon's threat, prophesied by Nausithoos, to "cover the city with an encircling mountain." Professor Shewan says that Homer must have invented this incident. The Phaeacians had enraged Poseidon (i) by robbing him of his legitimate victim, Odysseus, and (ii) by going too fast in their ships, which insulted the superiority of the Gods. "And so we owe to the poet's imagination, thus kindled, the incidents of the prophecy of Nausithoos, the petrifaction of the ship and the origin of the mountain that shut out Scheria from its interior." This is all very well, but surely one cannot so conveniently draw the line between real and imaginary; to be consistent one must accept or reject the story *in toto*. Experience shows that even the most

apparently fantastic episodes of an epic may be founded
upon fact; and in this very case it seems that the incident
of the petrified ship may after all be tracked down to an
origin in some ship-shaped islet or rock. "Here," writes
Stanley Casson,[23] who accepts the identification of Scheria
and Corfu, "to me, at least, is a valuable hint. Any such
rock, anywhere in the world, at any age, would give rise
to the local legend that once upon a time it was a ship
that was struck by some magician into a rock. Such it must
always have been called by the most ancient Corfiots. A
poet goes to Corfu from Ithaca, sees the rock, hears the
story, and at once places it in his story as the Phaeacian
ship that was smitten by Poseidon." What then, of
Poseidon's threat to cover the town with a mountain?
How can we logically reject that? But it is necessary before
considering that question to try and establish the meaning
of the phrase: ὄρος πόλει ἀμφικαλύψειν. (*Od.* 8. 569) Translations vary. "Shroud our city with a high mountain"
(T. E. Shaw), "Fling a mountain about our city" (A. T.
Murray), "Cover the town with a great encircling mountain" (Victor Bérard). At any rate it does not mean that
Poseidon was going to crush the town by hurling a mountain down upon it; on the contrary he was going to inflict
the more subtle punishment of surrounding it with a wall
of mountains in such a way as to prevent the Phaeacian
ships from getting to the sea. But since the Phaeacians
are essentially a sea-power and their commercial prosperity
depends on the swift passage of their ships from port to

port, the encircling mountain would certainly "crush" the city in the sense of annihilating their means of livelihood. In most of the translations of the word ἀμφικαλύψειν the sense of death is implied; "over-shadow," "enshroud," "obscure" are typical renderings. Had Homer made Poseidon threaten, in so many words to crush the whole town by actually hurling a mountain down upon it, we should have known at once that he must have been referring to a tradition of some volcanic eruption, a Pompeian disaster. But he does not. Instead he tells of this curiously "round-about" cataclysm. Even so it seems quite on the cards that he was referring indirectly, and in a manner flattering to the omnipotence of Poseidon, to some disaster which he knew from tradition or personal observation to be true. If so, Corfu again seems inadequate as the original of Scheria.

Neither Corfu nor Crete, then, seem entirely satisfactory; and so we are forced to return to speculation about the relationship between Scheria and Plato's Atlantis which, as we have tried to show, cannot very well be derived from any tradition or mixture of traditions surviving in Greece as late as Plato. The superficial resemblance between the two islands is confirmed in the work of those who believe that both Scheria and Plato's Atlantis must be equated with yet another ancient city, Tartessos, perhaps the Tarshish of the Bible and approximately the modern Cadiz. The exponents of this theory[24] admit that Tartessos may originally have been colonized by Crete but see in the topography

83

common to both Homer and Plato a direct reflection of the rich and brilliant Phoenician city beyond the pillars of Hercules which was captured and sacked by the Carthaginians in 533 B.C. Even if we eliminate the obviously Minoan elements in both accounts there are still resemblances, and it is interesting to note there seem to be a correspondence of those very points which might be considered as fundamental, or parts of a "plot" derived from ancient tradition. Thus both Atlantis and Scheria are in the extreme west of the world and both are threatened with a great cataclysm for displeasing Poseidon. Homer does not actually tell us whether Poseidon carried out his threat to punish his rebellious descendants by "shrouding them with an encircling mountain" or whether the sacrifice of bulls ordained by Alcinous succeeded in appeasing the angry God; but it may well be that Homer knew of the fate which overtook Scheria and because it was irrelevant to the development of his epic, decided that it would be artistically better to leave the tale unfinished and concentrate on the fortunes of his hero in Ithaca.

But even assuming that Homer did know a tradition of a western isle overwhelmed in a great cataclysm, how can we reconcile that with the tradition that Plato knew, about an island "covered" by the ocean? Superficially of course the two accounts are different though it is perhaps significant that Poseidon the sea god plays an important part in both; but there is one small piece of external information which suggests a more real connection. In 1898 a cable-laying vessel, looking for a broken cable between Brest and Cape Cod discovered that the sea-floor 1,000 miles north of the Azores at a depth of 3,100 metres consisted of high peaks and mountainous valleys. Special sounds dragged along the bottom brought up fragments of vitreus lava which could only have solidified in that particular form under atmospheric pressure; yet they must have been plunged beneath the water shortly after cooling because the process of erosion had not planed down the surface and levelled out the sharp hollows and protuberances of the rock. From this data a few geologists of eminence,[25] agreeing about the volcanic nature of this part of the Atlantic bed, have come to the conclusion that there must have been an island such as Plato's island existing in the Atlantic long after the opening of the straits of Gibraltar.

It is a romantic possibility, that the voices of those who to-day speak to their friends in America by trans-Atlantic telephone may be whispering between the ancient weed-covered towers of the dead city of Atlantis. But the question is: at the time of the sinking of this volcanic island did any species of man exist sufficiently *sapiens* to be capable of transmitting the story of the cataclysm to posterity? That is the crux of the whole scientific problem. At any rate it suggests a real though remote connection between the sinking of Plato's Atlantis and Poseidon's threat in Homer to shroud the Phaeacians with a mountain. Perhaps Scheria is indeed Atlantis, the island beyond the Pillars of Hercules, and Homer knew of a somewhat different version of the same tradition which Plato was later to shape into the story of the *Timaeus* and *Critias*. But nothing definite emerges from the enquiry and we are never out of the region of grand speculation. The only legitimate conclusion is a negative one; that the opponents of the Atlantean theory are not justified in the dogmatic assertion that Plato was the first writer to mention Atlantis.

So far, then, the position is this. The fundamental as well as the superficial resemblance between Homer's Scheria and Plato's Atlantis points to a tradition before Plato. The story could not have descended to Plato through Greek tradition and must therefore have come from Egypt. If we dismiss as bogus documentation Plato's own assertion that the story came to him through documents preserved in his family, it seems likely that he heard the tale himself when travelling in Egypt. It is doubtful if Homer's version can be *entirely* based upon his knowledge, direct or indirect, of Minoan Crete or Mycenaean Corfu, though it is evident that Scheria owes *something* to both. Hence the ground for speculating whether the Homeric story is not a fabric of Minoan and Mycenaean memories woven on a framework of some much older story about an island beyond the Pillars of Hercules.

We come now to the principal part of K. T. Frost's argument. Granted that Plato got his tradition from Egypt, does that story represent a composite picture of Minoan history as recorded by the Egyptians?

The Story of Atlantis

The case is well argued with a wealth of corroborative detail, but here again it is spoilt by the new theory of the fall of Knossos; for if Knossos was not after all invaded by "Athenians," but destroyed by an earthquake, no tradition of a Greek victory over the aggressive island power could have existed in Egypt. And it is just this part of the Atlantis story which is most open to suspicion for other reasons; the obviously Utopian character of the Greek state, the important link with the Republic, and the curious point, already referred to, that Plato has to get rid of the Greeks in the final catastrophe which destroys Atlantis. The internal evidence alone is sufficient to show conclusively that Plato himself was responsible for the account of the prehistoric Greek civilization and the part played by them in the story of Atlantis. But there is another big objection to Frost's argument. On the face of it, it is unlikely that only 600 years after the supposed collapse of Cretan civilization, an Egyptian priest should assure a Greek traveller that Atlantis-Crete had disappeared 8,000 years before. 600 years is a long time—it would take us back to the Middle Ages—but it is surely not long enough for tradition to transport a "floating" Crete 1,000 miles west of its proper site, beyond the Pillars of Hercules, enlarge it to the size of Libya and Asia Minor, and predate it by 8,000 years. Frost admits the difficulty himself, but overcomes it by stating dogmatically that it is scientifically certain that no such island as described by Plato could have existed since palaeolithic days. Another difficulty is that Minoan Crete was well known in Egypt both before and after the fall of Knossos. Now it is hardly likely that, even after the attack on Egypt by the Mycenaean-Achaean sea-raiders, the intercourse between them should have ceased so completely that the Egyptian priests and historians could entirely disassociate the history and geography of Crete. In Palestine[26] descendants of the sea-raiders defeated by Ramases still preserved memories of their Cretan origin; there was actually a settlement of Cretan refugees at Gaza, not much more than 200 miles from the Nile delta and Sais itself, and it is difficult to believe that they kept entirely to themselves. Trading caravans must have brought their story to Egypt.

But if we admit that there is a connection between Atlantis and Minoan Crete and that Plato's story may, through Egypt, have embodied certain detached memories of the palace of Minos it is surely simpler to accept the theory, recently advanced by Professor Shewan[27] that the story of Atlantis had long been familiar in Egyptian tradition whether or not it was real in fact; but being somewhat bare of detail the popular imagination gradually embellished it with contemporary reports of Crete during the palace period. The Atlantis story, despite the fact that Plato left it unfinished, has a certain character of fundamental completeness that suggests a framework already existing before he handled it, a "plot" too true to be the result of history getting mixed up. Indeed it is largely this apparent truthfulness which has enabled the story to survive the muddle and mystification of the Platonic dialogues, caused by Plato's failure to achieve his philosophic purpose in writing them. The further back we go the less inclined writers seem to have been to "invent" plots or even to use contemporary material when they had at hand a glorious stock of perfectly good "living" myth and history from which to choose. And in the present case a traditional plot seems the more likely when we realize that there are a great many other features in the Atlantis story to upset Frost's simple equation: Plato's Atlantis=condensed Cretan history+a flood legend. Also, there is some external evidence, based on certain resemblances between Pre-Minoan civilization in Crete which seems to have been inhabited as early as 10,000 B.C. by Mediterranean peoples, and the neolithic cultures of the Biscay region, to indicate that elements of western culture may have reached the eastern Mediterranean before the bronze age. It has even been suggested[28] that neolithic Crete was a colony of Atlantis. But that is a question to be considered in another place.

To sum up and return to Scheria. It has been argued that K. T. Frost was right in drawing attention to the Minoan features of Homer's Scheria and Plato's Atlantis, but mistaken in his conclusion that Atlantis is *simply* condensed memories of Minoan Crete disassociated from their geographical location and joined up with a flood legend. The counter-suggestion is that Plato's Atlantis represents essentially an ancient Egyptian or possibly Cretan story, perhaps going back as far as the stone age and barren of detail; but that this nucleus is padded out with later memories of the great period of Minoan civilization and a number of other accessory details deliberately introduced into the story by Plato himself.

(5)

The case for Atlantis has suffered very much from a slavishly fundamental belief in a traditional basis for every detail of the Platonic account; for it is obvious to anyone who keeps a reasonably open mind that a great deal of the incidental detail in the story is due to intelligent observation on Plato's part and to imaginative use of contemporary material at his disposal.

An enormous variety of sources has been suggested, and although most of them, taken separately, are open to doubt, collectively they cannot be ignored even by the most pious believer in the "truthfulness" of Plato.

(i) The city of Atlantis owes something to Babylon. The regular mathematical plan, the plain, the irrigation system and the hydraulic works are strongly reminiscent of the Babylonian plain. Plato could have got his knowledge from Herodotus, Zenophon or Ctesias.[29]

(ii) The description of the great naval works of Atlantis were perhaps inspired by personal observation of the preparations of Dionysius I at Syracuse to defend Sicily from the Carthaginian menace.[30] Plato visited Sicily twice, at the age of 40 and again 20 years later. This and (i) shows the danger of over-emphasizing the "purely Minoan" elements of Atlantis.

(iii) In the materialistic, wealthy and luxurious state of Atlantis there is a distinct trace of the "gorgeous east," which would seem to Plato both attractive and decadent, or at any rate sufficiently remote from the classic severity of Athenian civilization to make an obvious contrast which would both point his moral and adorn his tale. The architecture of the citadel of Atlantis suggests the pavilions of the Arabian Nights. It stands to Athenian architecture as Brighton Pavilion to that of Regency England, stimulated by Byron's oriental poems and the general cult of the exotic. The metals with which Plato's Atlantis is so lavishly adorned have no place in the Atlantic island conceived by sympathetic geologists. Atlantis, if it existed, was a Stone-Age culture. Neither history nor archaeology knows anything of orichalc, the mountain copper which glowed like fire. Either Plato used a term which in his day meant something different to designate his own fantastic metal or else it is a metal which is no longer known. The name is found before Plato.[31]

(iv) The attempt to identify the Atlantean cult of Poseidon, practised by the kings of the federation of Atlas, with the solar cult of the Aztecs has resulted in the printing of a good deal of nonsense. One thing only is certain. The religious practices of the kings of Atlantis are intended by Plato to strengthen the contrast between the ideal

Greeks and the barbarian islanders. Practices of this kind had died out in Greece by the 5th century. The source of the description is not clear, but it probably represents a compound of practices derived from various mystery cults. Bachofer[32] characterises the custom of sitting round by night on the ground as a return to the principle of the primitive matriarchate, according to which justice was an attribute of mother earth, Ge or Demeter. There is also an evident relation with the Orphic mysteries, of which the essential features were known to Plato and dated from the 6th and 7th centuries,[33] especially in its sacramental and "ghostly" character, and in the obviously symbolic nature of the ritual. The central ritual act of the wine-drinking may also connect it with the ritual practice in the Greek mystery at Eleusis near Athens, where there was a communion with sacred flour and a divine drink, originating possibly in the consumption of the flesh and blood of sacrificial animals.[34] A Cretan character is stamped on the bull-chasing incident; wherever the influence of Minoan civilization was felt the hunting of the sacred bull was part of the sacrificial ritual.[35] Lastly, there is the possibility of Egyptian influence, not to be overlooked if Plato got other parts of the story from Egypt; but it is sufficient to note that Herodotus thought that the Orphic ritual, which had features in common with Osiris worship, was of Egyptian origin.[36] Osiris was alternatively known in the form of Apis, the bull-god, usually slain sacrificially while the animal was still strong.[37]

Apparently then, the Atlantean cult of Poseidon is a

compound with certain recognizable ingredients. Did Plato compound them himself, or were the elements absorbed one by one from different sources at different times as the Atlantis tradition strove by a process of natural selection to continue its growth along the wall of time? The truth is probably somewhere between the two; some elements may have been in the story before it reached Plato, others may have been introduced by him.

(v) Professor Taylor thinks that Plato's account of the end of Atlantis was inspired by the disastrous earthquake and tidal wave which devastated the Achaean coast in 373 B.C.

This may very well have set his mind working on the theme of "acts of God," but it can hardly have served as a basis for a story about the swamping of a great island. If we must connect it with the Atlantis story, it is surely more likely to have given rise to Plato's account of the great floods and earthquakes which (*Critias* 112) denuded the Athenian acropolis.

(vi) Plato probably concocted the story of the part played by the prehistoric Greeks in the fortunes of Atlantis, for three reasons:

(*a*) The detailed description of the prehistoric Athens seems to be without traditional foundation. The account of its political and social organization merely illustrates the principles laid down by Plato himself in the *Republic*, to which the *Critias* is linked. It is essentially Utopian in character; and the drowning of the victorious Greeks in

93

the same catastrophe which overwhelmed their Atlantean rivals suggests that Plato wanted to get rid of them in order to account for the absence of any tradition in the Greece of his own day.

(*b*) There is no archaeological evidence for the existence of civilized Greeks in the peninsula before the first dynasty in Egypt. It would be quite natural for a Greek, lacking information about the past history of his own country, to endow his. ancestors with an ancient and honourable past, just as the English once traced their descent from the Trojans or the Emperor Haile Selassie from the Queen of Sheba. "Golden Age" speculations were always popular in classical literature.

(*c*) The general course of the war between the Athenians and the Atlanteans may be inspired by the Athenian resistance to Xerxes and Darius.[38] The point is that a small nation, if matched against forces superior in numbers and equipment, can win provided it is patriotic and has a sound morale.

(6)

It is evident then that, without looking too far afield, many features of Plato's story can be accounted for independently of any tradition. If we forget all that has been said already in favour of Atlantis being a full-grown tradition deliberately adapted by Plato to suit his philosophic purpose, it is possible to get the impression that the *Critias*

94

and *Timaeus* are merely the result of intelligent co-ordination of unrelated observations and memories derived from personal experience or from literature; sheer invention in fact. But the process of invention is not quite so simple as it sounds.

Anyone who has ever tried to "invent" a new plot, which is not based upon some particular combination of character and incident already known to the author from experience or second-hand, will be aware that however keen his powers of observation, however vivid his "imagination," it is extremely difficult to concoct one that is essentially different from certain general plots, such, for example, as "the eternal triangle" or "shipwreck on a desert island." Human activity is restricted by evolution and in time all its important manifestations become codified as recorded events which are continually recurring both in life and literature in a thousand modifications. So that the chances are that if a plot is a "new" one it will be also unimportant, too particular to be interesting outside a small section of people qualified to understand the "technique" it exhibits; and its lack of universal "human appeal" will probably result in an ephemeral life because it will have no enduring place in the collective psyche of mankind. The *Lost Horizon*, for instance, a novel which was widely hailed as a work of imagination with an original plot was in fact no more than a restatement in terms of contemporary problems of the story of Noah's Ark. What was original about the story was the treatment of the ark theme, and in that sense it was rightly

95

praised as a work of imagination. To find his essential plot, a varied assortment of creatures escaping from the flood of modern existence to a remote place where the rarefied air could safely preserve the relics of palmier days and transmit them to posterity, James Hilton had only to look up the book of *Genesis*. It is the same with most great works of the imagination, works which are on the grand scale besides being elaborate, dignified, and tragic; in short, epics. The *Iliad*, the Arthur story, *Beowulf*, the *Niebelungenlied*, the *Chanson de Roland* are all examples of epic stories; and they all have their "genesis," though, being closer to the events they record, they deal with legend in a more personal way, concentrating on the deeds of individual heroes for their main interest. In the *Critias* it is not necessary to remember that Plato says Solon wanted to write an epic on the Atlantis theme in order to recognize in it the quality of epic; it is elaborate, dignified and dramatic almost to the intensity of tragedy. It does not matter that it is written in scrappy prose and not in noble verse,[39] or that the narrative, as it stands, says nothing of individual heroes. The point is that the theme has epic proportions, deliberately treated according to the very unepical convention of the Platonic dialogue as an improving work for a sophisticated and literate public, and not intended, like the Homeric or Scandinavian epics, for stirring recitation on public occasions of importance.

Any attempt at rigid classification would be unjustified by the nature of the evidence; but at least it can be argued that the Atlantis story belongs to that type of noble and universal plot which in the past has given cause to look for a genesis in actual fact or in the tradition of history;[40] and as such it is legitimate to guess how it may have grown from an old tradition dating from the Stone Age to the perplexing mass of material which is ordered by Plato's artistry into the tragedy of Atlantis.

Gilbert Murray has shown[41] that the Greek epic should be regarded as a traditional book, based on some old poem or poems, and modified by subsequent generations to suit the changing times. The epic in its final form is a condensed mass of material representing compressed layers of history, the surface strata bearing the impress of the latest phase of civilization concerned in its formation and transmission, and deep down the marks of the earlier ages in which the nucleus or nuclei were shaped.

Now if we can regard the Atlantis story in this way, the question: "Did Atlantis really exist?" begins to assume its proper perspective. But there is an important difference between Plato's epic and the Homeric epics which must be referred to the very source of the material. If we contrast the story of Atlantis with that of the *Iliad* it is obvious that whereas both are works of art in the sense that they have been logically constructed, the Atlantis story has a unity, a centralized purpose, which the *Iliad* with its many digressions and episodes entirely lacks; in the case of the *Iliad* this lack of centralization is probably due to a lack of homogeneity in the original raw material,[42] consisting of several

97

unconnected lays in praise of tribal Gods somehow linked into a whole for the first time. It is a confluence of little streams derived from various sources and swollen into a great river; but the Atlantis story, so it seems, is derived from a single spring which, welling from the earth, has gradually grown into a river not through union with other streams, but by being fed by heavy rains; in other words there is one channel from source to mouth. This *origo* is an old tradition of an island in the far west destroyed in an ocean cataclysm; and the external evidence shows that it must (if the hypothesis is correct) have originated in the Stone Age. But from the very earliest times it must have been associated with some tribal god, perhaps a palaeolithic Poseidon, who caused the cataclysm and gave to the tradition a supernatural impulse which preserved it in the imagination of migrating peoples. The real Atlantis has nothing to do with metals. The description of orichalc plated walls and golden statues must be derived from Minoan and Mycenaean influences to which the story was subjected at successive periods of its later development. Still later, in the period of Greek influence upon Egypt, other features began to appear, details derived from Babylon and Greece itself. And finally perhaps, in Plato's day, the story of the flood which devastated prehistoric Attica may be an Egyptian version of the cataclysm which actually ravaged the Achaean coast in 373 B.C. It might on the other hand be one of Plato's own insertions, in which case it would have been incorporated with a number of other fruits of his observation including memories of the harbour at Syracuse, the whole "touched up" and coloured with imaginative artistry.

The fact that people have all along been very sceptical about any real foundation for the Atlantis story means very little. As an example of how time alters opinions there is the Arthur legend, the history of which resembles that of Atlantis in many respects. Both have excited wild speculations arising out of their universal diffusion through every language and culture, and the authenticity of both has been widely suspected. For years Geoffrey of Monmouth in his history of Britain was thought, like Plato, to have invented a "noble lie"[43] and the *British Book* from which he claimed to have got his material was held to be a myth as baseless as Solon's epic poem. From Caxton, who wrote in his preface to Mallory's *Morte D'Arthur:* "Divers men hold opinion that there was no such Arthur and that books as be made of him be but feigned and fables" to George Saintsbury, who talked of the "Arthurian invention," there is the same scepticism. But few now doubt that there was a 6th century historical Arthur with a knowledge of Roman warfare who fought to maintain the independence of the West of England against the Saxon invaders; and there are a number of scholars who think that Geoffrey's *British Book* may have existed as well. The detection of accretions in the final story has not altered the basic fact of Arthur's existence. Merlin drops out, the Round Table goes by the board and most of the knights with their suspiciously mediaeval chivalry and errantry are found to be mere gate-crashers. But despite the pretended exhumation of his bones

99

by some monks of Glastonbury who wished to disillusion the credulous and expectant Celts, Arthur lives on, a historical personage, in fabled Avallon. There Morgan la Fay tends his wounds against the day of his return, and there some think (strange coincidence if it were true) that Arthur is surrounded by curious relics of another equally famous Otherworld, the sunk Atlantis. Perhaps it was indeed to Plato's island that Morgan rowed Arthur after the battle of Camlan, but so wrapped in Celtic sea-mists out in the West that it seems a different place.

(7)

One blind alley leads to another and analogy is as tempting as it is treacherous. Earlier in this chapter Coleridge's unwelcome visitor from Porlock was wantonly dragged in with reference to the broken *Critias*. Now that we have worked round to the question of imagination and tradition, it looks as if Coleridge might be of some use after all, if only to cast doubt on the "baseless fabric" theory which maintains that the Atlantis story is merely the result of a conscious and deliberate ordering of Plato's own experience into an "original " whole.

It has been suggested that the Atlantis story has the proportions of an embryonic epic. The contents of the *Critias* has certain curious points of contact with Coleridge's *Kubla Khan*, and a cautious comparison of the two accounts is interesting for its own sake, if for no other reason. But first the differences which prevent an exact parallel should be noted. Broadly, the *Critias* appears to be the result of "taking thought," whereas Coleridge's poem springs from an ordering of the subconscious mind arrived at during an opium trance. That is not to admit that *Kubla Khan* exhibits the raw subconscious material in the same way as a surréalist poem, but merely to distinguish it from the result of the rational method of composition. Secondly, the *Critias* bears the stamp of a philosophical and mathematical mind largely conditioned by the classical age in which Plato lived. *Kubla Khan* is the effusion of an intelligence fogged by opiates and naturally inclined to the romantic revolt from the neo-classicism of the Augustan poets. Lastly, the story of Atlantis is part of a moral fable, *Kubla Khan* is not. But, *mutatis mutandis*, the resemblances between the two stories are as curious as they are apparently fortuitous.[44]

(i) Both *Critias* and *Kubla Khan* are fragments of imaginative works on a large scale.

(ii) The city of Atlantis has the same oriental luxuriousness as the Pleasure Dome.

(iii) The Khan's "gardens bright with sinuous rills" are reminiscent of Poseidon's grove in Atlantis.

(iv) In *Kubla Khan* "twice five miles of fertile ground" were encompassed with walls and towers. The hill which Poseidon enclosed stood in a fertile plain and was also bounded by turreted walls.

(v) Both *Critias* and *Kubla Khan* contain a note of doom.

Amid the sound of the river Alph sinking in tumult to a
lifeless ocean

> Kubla heard from far
> Ancestral voices prophesying war!
> The shadow of the dome of Pleasure
> Floated midway on the waves . . .

The Atlanteans, too, must have heard the voice of their
divine ancestors, descendants of Poseidon, warning them of
the vengeance to come. Their shadow was upon the waters
of the Atlantic. . . .

Leaving Plato for the moment, let us consider what were
Coleridge's sources for *Kubla Khan*. The whole story is in
Professor Lowes' great book *The Road to Xanadu*. "The
web of creation, like the skein of life, is of mingled yarn,
conscious and unconscious inextricably intertwined . . .
and imaginative creation . . . is not one process but two—
an infinitely complex process in which conscious and
unconscious jointly operate. There is beyond gainsaying
the Deep Well, with its chaos of fortuitously blending
images, and there is likewise the Vision which sees shining
in and through the chaos of fortuitously blending images
the potential lines of form, and with the Vision the con-
trolling will, which gives to that potential beauty actuality."
He then goes on to show what were the actual sources of
Kubla Khan. Books, old books. Purchas's *Pilgrimage* and
Pilgrims, Bartram's *Enchanting Little Isle of Palms*, and
Bruce's *Travels in Abyssinia* to discover the sources of the
Nile. Add to these many odd reminiscences of his reading

from the mediaeval voyages and tales of Fortunate Isles, and we have *Kubla Khan* almost word for word, image for image. But what do we know of the genesis of the poem? What put the idea into Coleridge's head and set working the machinery of creation which Professor Lowes describes? Coleridge himself tells the story:

In the summer 1797 he had retired in ill-health to a lonely farmhouse near Porlock. In consequence of a "slight indisposition" an anodyne had been prescribed and from its effects he fell asleep in his chair when reading the following sentence in Purchas's *Pilgrimage*: "In Xaindu did Kublai Can build a stately palace, encompassing 16 miles of plaine grounde with a wall, wherin are fertile meadows, delightfulle streames, and all sorts of beasts of chase and game, and on the middest therof a sumptuous house of Pleasure, which may be moved from place to place." During his sleep he composed 200 or 300 lines of poetry, and on awakening he appeared to have a distinct recollection of the whole. He was eagerly writing it down, when he was interrupted, after he had committed to paper the fragments which now exists, by a man from Porlock who came to see him on business and detained him more than an hour; by the time he returned to his pen and paper the whole thing had faded from his mind and he was unable to remember sufficient to continue.

From this account it is evident that but for the sentence in Purchas, the "shaping spirit" could not have fished all the accessory images and associations out of the "deep well." The sentence in Purchas is not only the *fons et origo*, but also the kernel round which the accessory associations gathered. It is *Kubla Khan* "in a nutshell." "If anything ever bore the infallible marks of authenticity," says Professor Lowes, commenting on the extraordinary lack of "invention" revealed in a work so obviously imaginative "it is that dissolving panorama." What, then, of the *Critias*, in which so many elements could have been derived, consciously or unconsciously from Plato's own experience? The lesson to be drawn from *Kubla Khan*, which, as we have seen, in some respects resembles the description of Atlantis, is surely that the greater the number of memories and associations stored up in a work of imagination, the more reason there is to look for a definite kernel to give them corporate substance and to suggest, in the vitally important first instance, the possibilities of associating a lot of stray minutiae.

To sum up. The conclusion is that Atlantis represents a traditional story incorporating a nucleus derived from the Stone Age; that this story reached Plato in a comparatively undeveloped state and was enlarged and adapted by him to contrast in as many ways as possible with his ideal state. There is no reason to reject Plato's statement that the story came from Egypt; especially since he probably visited the country himself. But it is just possible that his oral source may have been committed to some lost book; in which case it is amusing to speculate whether, if the great library at Alexandria had survived for the inspection of modern research scholars like Professor Lowes, some old books of travels, perhaps dating back beyond the time of Herodotus might not have turned up to prove once and for all that the legend of Atlantis is no more a baseless fabric than Coleridge's *Kubla Khan*. There are in fact two such lacunae mentioned in classical literature.[45] The lost *Argonautica* of Dionysius of Mitylene mentioned by Diodorus and the unidentified author Statius Sebosus in Pliny. But we know nothing of these books. And so, for further evidence, we have to turn to the modern scientific theories of the Atlantic isle based on the teachings of geology, ethnology and archaeology.

THROUGH A GLASS DARKLY

(1)

We come now to the scientific search for Atlantis, upon which Aunt Jane was unhappily engaged when she went off her head. This was due, it may be remembered, to the multiplicity and conflict of the Atlantean theories, for without devising some drastic method of elimination the layman who is unversed in the recent progress of geology, ancient history and ethnography is unlikely to be able to discriminate sufficiently to steer a critical course in the midst of them. The search is further complicated by the fact that, strictly speaking, the "scientists" are not all ultimately looking for the same thing. Some, the philologists and archaeologists, are in search of a lost civilization to correspond in detail with Plato's Atlantis; while others, the majority of geologists, ethnographers and botanists, are looking for an Atlantis to provide an explanation for some curious facts about the Ice Age, the distribution of flora and fauna and the mystery of racial origins. For the former group Atlantis is an end: for the latter it is merely the means to an end. On the whole the latter group, which can see the problem with some detachment, is the more reliable. But in either case the ocean of prehistory is so vast and the equipment for charting it so inadequate that it is easy to be persuaded, like the early Irish Saints, that the first island to emerge from the uncertain mists is the desired terrestrial paradise. Atlantean researches have been aptly described as an "archipelago of hypotheses."[1]

In modern times there are about eight main hypotheses to choose from. Atlantis in America, in North Africa, and in Nigeria; Atlantis as an island in the Atlantic Ocean; Atlantis as Tartessos; Karst's theory of a twofold Atlantis; Gidon's theory of the land subsidences between Ireland and Brittany in the Bronze Age; and the theory that Plato's Atlantis represents a memory of the flooding of the Mediterranean basin.

(2)

Atlantis was first thought to be America about sixty years after the discovery of the New World seemed to have confirmed all the classical tales about islands in the extreme west of the world. The identification was further strengthened by the discovery that the native name for Mexico was Aztlan.[2] But in Elizabethan times the interest in the newly found Atlantis was merely incidental to projects for seeking the north-west passage to Cathay. Sir Humphrey Gilbert and many other contemporary geographers and sailors, including Peter Martyr and Ortelius, maintained that if Atlantis-America had been partially overwhelmed by a cataclysm there must be navigable waters about its northern coasts.[3] This theory, however, does not seem to have been accepted everywhere. Montaigne, writing about

1580, was perfectly ready to believe that Atlantis was overwhelmed in a cataclysm, but he was extremely sceptical about it being America. "There is no great apparance the said island should be the new world we have lately discovered; for, it well-nigh touched *Spaine* and it were an incredible effect of inundation, to have removed the same more than 1200 leagues, as we see it is." (Florio). Yet at the beginning of the 17th century Francis Bacon still seems to have accepted the identification of Atlantis and America, and he uses it as the basis for his Utopian island in the *New Atlantis*. His account of the Great Atlantis, though presented as fiction, may very well be his own version of the probable facts underlying Plato's story. Most of the Platonic story, the governor of the New Atlantis tells his Peruvian visitors, is probably poetical or fabulous. The Great Atlantis included Mexico and Peru, powerful central American kingdoms, which flourished 3,000 years ago. They were rich in arms and ships, and they were aggressively imperialistic. From Mexico an expedition sailed east through the straits of Gibraltar into the Mediterranean. They, in the governor's opinion, were those Atlanteans of whom Solon learnt from the Egyptian priests, for the expedition never returned to Mexico. At the same time an expedition sailed west from Peru and discovered the New Atlantis (called Bensalem). The Peruvians had better fortune than the Mexicans. The king of Bensalem was an enlightened monarch and after winning a bloodless victory over his would-be conquerors he spared their lives.

But less than a hundred years later the imperialism of the Great Atlantis was punished in a series of earthquakes, "so as marvel you not at the thin population of America nor the rudeness and ignorance of the people: for you must account your inhabitants of America as a very young people, younger 1,000 years at the least, than the rest of the world; for that there was so much time between the universal flood and their particular inundation."

Atlantis has continued to be related to America right down to modern times. In the 18th century Buffon and Conte Carli, and in the 19th Alexander de Humboldt and Jacob Kruger, contributed to the theory. But nowadays its advocates have shifted their ground somewhat. Instead of maintaining that Atlantis was geographically identical with the present American continent, they prefer to argue that America is merely a continuation of a much larger continent, the eastern or Atlantean part of which is now submerged under the Atlantic. In its later stage, therefore, the American theory converges upon the theory of Atlantis as an island continent in the Atlantic, and it can be conveniently left over to be discussed in relation to the work of Lewis Spence and others.

(3)

During the last seventy years, North Africa, which is still rather an unknown quantity from an archaeological point of view despite rapid colonization, has been an important hunting ground for the Atlantean explorers. The rush began in 1874 when the French archaeologist Félix Berlioux staked out his claim to have found Atlantis at the foot of some high mountains in the Moroccan Atlas, nearly opposite the Canary Islands. Here, according to Berlioux, was the ancient city of the Atlanteans, which corresponds to Cerne, the capital of a people called the Atlantes described in the *Historical Library* of Diodorus Siculus (See Appendix C). Berlioux believed that Atlantis, the city of the *Critias*, was not on an island at all but merely the capital of the vast empire which according to Plato stretched from the Atlantic to Etruria in the north, and to Egypt in the south. While the Atlanteans were being driven back both on land and sea by the combined forces of Egyptians and Phoenicians in the Eastern Mediterranean, a people called the Gaetulae, Hamitic ancestors of the present Berber tribes, advanced upon the capital, Atlantis, and destroyed it. But a few of the Atlanteans survived as a subject race living among their conquerors, and their descendants, thought Berlioux, are still recognizable in the blonde blue-eyed natives sometimes encountered in the mountains of Algeria.

This theory is the basis of Pierre Benoit's novel *L'Atlantide*, which converts Tin Hinan, the legendary matriarch of the Berbers, into an exotic autocrat called Antinea, the last of the descendants of Poseidon and Clito, who rules over the fortress remains of the Lost City. The novel describes how two Frenchmen penetrated into the fastnesses of the Ahaggar Massif in the central Sahara, and found Atlantis.

Through a Glass Darkly

More recently Claude Roux argued that in the post-glacial period of the Quaternary age North West Africa was a fertile peninsula bounded by great shallow lagoons which stretched from the Atlantic and the Mediterranean to the southern Atlas. This mountainous peninsula was extremely fertile and thickly populated; flora and fauna abounded. But in the course of many millenniums, while successive colonisations of Berbers, Carthaginians and Romans were taking place, the physical character of the land was gradually changing. The lagoons receded towards the coast leaving lakes and salt-marshes, the traces of which can still be seen in the Schotts and Sebkas of Algeria and Tunisia. At the same time began a "reign of sand," and life and vegetation could no longer exist. "Atlantis " became a memory.

Roux's theory couples the mystery of Atlantis with that of Glozel near Vichy, where in 1926 the discovery of some clay tablets and inscribed pebbles associated with Palaeolithic objects found previously in south-west France and Portugal as well as in Morocco and in the Sahara, led Professor Saloman Reinach to assert that alphabetic and syllabic writing was known to a small priestly class in the West centuries before it was known in the East, but that this civilization was destroyed by invaders from the North, with the result that alphabetic writing had to be relearnt at a later date, this time from the East. "I wonder then," says Roux, "whether the Glozel mystery does not tend to merge into the mystery of Atlantis, and whether the regions round the Pillars of Hercules have not in prehistoric and protohistoric times played an important part in civilization . . . Further researches in France, in Spain and in North Africa will prove perhaps that this hypothesis is well-founded, at the same time enabling the Atlantean problem to be cleared up."

But the Glozel affair is not yet settled. The writings are generally thought to be bogus, and Roux's theory is therefore in suspension.

Another champion of the Saharan Atlantis is Count Byron Kuhn de Prorok. In his *Mysterious Sahara* (Murray, 1930) he describes how he discovered traces of the Lost Atlantis in the desert, and more recently (*In Search of Lost Worlds*, Muller, 1935) he gives an account of further and more dramatic finds. But his discoveries, sensational though they seem to the lay intelligence, do not appear to have impressed the professional archaeologists very deeply. Comparison of De Prorok's account of his expeditions and the subsequent "official" comment upon them throws an interesting light upon the relation of romantic field archaeology to the archaeology of the Museum.

The author of *In Search of Lost Worlds* frankly prefers the "unstable side of archaeology" to comfortable excavation of sites in friendly civilized places; he wants adventure, danger and romance. Hence the 1925–26 expedition to the Ahaggar Massif in search of Tin Hinan or Antinea, legendary matriarch of the hostile Tuareg tribes, buried perhaps in the remote desert fastnesses. This conception of the purpose of the expedition, which started ostensibly to search for prehistoric sites and to study Tuareg origins, plainly owed a good deal to Benoit's romance; but it also coincided with De Prorok's inclination to seek out the old caravan routes of the Phoenician traders. The notion fitted in with a vague theory of a vast prehistoric migration, traces of which he had already found in the Libyan desert, at Sima, in the Fayum, in the Tripolitan Sahara and "even so far as the Red Sea to the east and the Atlantic to the west." Later he found links of the same chain in Yucatan and Central America. "To the north and south of the line so marked, the workmanship (of the prehistoric implements) had different characteristics; but we found similar specimens, and traces of this highly individualized prehistoric folk by hundreds and thousands, stretching to Ethiopia and the British Sudan."

"I wondered and I still wonder, if ultimately there may be a definite link with the Atlanteans along this line; the wonder has at least stirred me to make succeeding expeditions."

In his search for the Tuareg matriarch he was not disappointed. The expedition duly penetrated into the Ahaggar country. At the court of the Sultan they induced the Court historian to tell them the full story of Tin Hinan, and by intelligent deduction from this story they managed to determine in which direction the tomb was likely to lie. An advance party set out to search for it and eventually found, at the confluence of two dry rivers, a high circular structure which they decided to excavate, notwithstanding the danger of being caught in the act by Tuareg tribesmen. In it they found precious stones and gold pieces. There were also bracelets and anklets, a couch of wood, and—the *pièce de résistance*—a skeleton. "The skeleton was lying on its side, and at the head a statuette, easily recognizable as being of the Aurignacian period; a squat crude image of a steatopygic goddess which we promptly named 'the Libyan Venus'." The skull, when measured, proved to be that of a woman . . . Tin Hinan, no doubt. There was an exciting moment when, in the middle of the excavations, some sinister-looking tribesman arrived and adopted a threatening attitude; but evidently they were unaware that the tomb of their legendary ancestress was in the process of being desecrated, for the excavators managed somehow to calm their suspicions, and afterwards continued with the work.

When M. Reygasse, the official archaeologist of the party, came up with the rest of the caravan, he said:

"We have made history, you and I, De Prorok ! . . . We have made history! We have changed all the conceptions of the Ahaggar!

"You must realise," he continued, his voice a little impeded by his anxious heart, "this is vast treasure. The tomb of Tin Hinan. We have found it! *Vive la France!*"

All this must be contrasted with what followed when the relics of Tin Hinan, hot from the sands of the Sahara, lay exposed to the cold scrutiny of the Museum experts.

It was not at all certain, the report stated,[4] that this tomb was really the tomb of Tin Hinan at all, for in any case she was a person more legendary than historic. "What is certain," runs the comment, "is that among the innumerable dry stone monuments that strew the Ahaggar, Count de Prorok has opened one which is the tomb of an Ahaggar dignitary."

Recently, however, this noncommittal view has been modified by further researches on the site by M. Reygasse.[5]

"It is readily conceivable that in the 4th century of our era some Ahaggar knight, a descendant of Tin Hinan, if you like, atavistically came under the influence of Rome, maintaining relations with the Roman-Punic traders of Leptis Magna, Sidamus and Carthage. There traders engaged in trans-Saharan traffic had need of him and he of them. He sold them his protection and established on his territory a way station. Thus one might interpret the monument of Tin Hinan—a stage on the road to the country of the Blacks."

Also in 1926 the geologist Paul Borchardt claimed to have found Atlantis in the region which was formerly Little Syrta in the Gulf of Gabes. From the Arab name of this region, the Ham Mam, Borchardt deduced that the salt lake Schott El Hammeina was once called the "Lake of the Atlantes." This lake was also known in historical times as Lake Tritonis, associated in legend with the Greek merman Triton, son of Poseidon and Amphitrite who according to Hesiod dwelt with his parents in a golden

115

palace under the sea. The connection seemed to Borchardt a significant one, for Lake Tritonis contained near its seaward side an island called Poseidon's island which he considered to be the same as Herodotus' Island of Phla with its temple of Athena.

Mount Atlas, according to Borchardt, whose theory is largely based on the supposition that the geographical ideas of the ancient world require very careful interpretation, was not in Algeria but in the Ahaggar Massif; there lived the race of the Libyan "Attala" as described in Herodotus, and Borchardt tried to relate the names of Poseidon's sons as given by Plato to names actually current among the tribes living in that part of the world to-day. The Pillars of Hercules, he thought, were not mountains on either side of the straits of Gibraltar but actual pillars of a temple of Hercules.

In general Borchardt considered that the mineral richness of the Schott country bears out the description in Plato of the richness of Atlantis and that the mysterious "oreichalkos" might well have been an alloy of copper and zinc, hence yellow copper or brass. The local stone, too, seemed to him to account for the variegated colour of Atlantean buildings. He considered that the "brass " Atlantean citadel was reflected both in Homer's Palace of Alcinous and in the "City of Brass" in the Tales of the Thousand and One Nights, some of which might have originated in Tunisian legend. An ancient fortress which he discovered near Gabes seemed to him to be an actual remnant of the prehistoric city. Unfortunately this fortress was subsequently proved to have been of Roman origin.

Undeterred by this reverse, Albert Hermann, another Tunisian protagonist, continued to look for Atlantis in Southern Tunisia. Working on similar lines to Borchardt, Hermann discovered another site for Atlantis, a depressed hamlet called Rhelissia situated near the mouth of the old river Tritonis. Here he found traces of ancient irrigation works planned on a considerable scale and with an ingenuity quite beyond the scope of the Rhelissians themselves; the general character of the ground reminded him of Plato's description of Atlantis.

Hermann based this attribution upon his conclusion that Plato's account in the Critias incorporated three fundamental errors.

(i) The Atlantic sea in the time of Solon was the name for the Tunisian Schott (Borchardt). The name Atlantic was not used to denote the Ocean before the time of Herodotus; but Plato only understood it in the modern sense, thus misinterpreting the tradition.

(ii) Plato was wrong in assigning 9,000 years before Solon as the date for the overwhelming of Atlantis. He was really thinking of the period immediately preceding that of Theseus, *i.e.* 14th or 13th century B.C.

(iii) The interpreter through whom Solon conversed with the priest of Sais had to translate Egyptian measures into their Greek equivalent. Egyptian schoinos were convertible into Greek stadia at the rate of 30 stadia to 1 schoinos. The interpreter had therefore to multiply the schoinos by 30 in order to arrive at the equivalent number of stadia.

Now the width of one of the canals, given by Plato at 300 feet "to allow the passage of a large vessel," is exactly 30 times the width actually required to permit the passage of an ancient vessel, which would not be more than 10 feet wide at the most. It is significant that this number 30 is also the common factor of all the other dimensions *given in feet*, for the town, the temple of Poseidon and the canals. From this Hermann concluded that owing to a slip on the part of the interpreter, who confused feet with stadia, a number of the measurements were accidentally multiplied by 30 giving an entirely false impression of the real proportions of Atlantis.

On this assumption the whole island of Atlantis, which according to Plato's figures, was the size of Libya and Asia Minor, would have been no larger than Tunisia; in the same way the fertile plain becomes a little sand-flat in the Schott El Djerid, the citadel itself covers only the area of a medium sized oasis 700–800 metres in diameter, while the huge sanctuary of Poseidon is scaled down to a modest temple 3 metres high.

The wider implications of Hermann's theory become clear in his latest book, *Unsere Ahnen und Atlantis* (Berlin 1934); here he restates his belief that we must look for Atlantis in Tunisia. But he thinks of it not as an indigenously developed civilization but as a colony, a stage in the transmission of the elements of a high culture to the Eastern Mediterranean. This culture says Hermann, came originally from Friesland, where lived a great civilization which colonized most of western Europe. The Frisian period lasted until the late Bronze Age and was responsible among other prehistoric monuments for the megaliths at Carnac and Stonehenge. This, of course, conflicts with the generally accepted theory that civilization came from East to West.

(4)

A less sensational hypothesis is that of the African explorer Leo Frobenius, according to whom Atlantis was part of Nigeria, in the Yoruba country between the loop of the Niger and the corresponding coastline. In the report of his third African voyage (*I. Band: Aus den Truemmern des Klassischen altertums.*) Frobenius wrote: "I therefore claim to have thus recovered Atlantis, the exchange centre of Western civilization, situated beyond the Pillars of Hercules; the Atlantis of which we are told by Solon that it was the site of Poseidon's fortress; that a flourishing vegetation covered it, that tree-like plants furnished food, drinks and balsams (the palm-oil tree); that there flourished the rapidly withering 'fruit tree' (banana) and pleasant condiments (pepper); that elephants lived there; that the country produced copper (as it actually did behind the Yoruba mountains until recently), that the natives wore dark-blue

119

(tree-indigo) robes, and that they had a somewhat alien architecture (saddle-shaped roofs made of palm leaves). I therefore consider the Yoruba country, a prolific and extremely rich tropical country, intersected all along its coasts and on the banks of the Niger by an infinite number of lagoons and canals, and well described in its essential detail by Plato's story, as having been Atlantis. I consider it as having been the country of Poseidon's descendants, whom the Yorubas called Olokon, the domain of a people of whom Solon said 'that they had extended their domination also to Egypt and the Tyrrhenian sea.' We have found the seafaring and warlike nation of the 13th century before our era. We have found this intermediary between Western and Eastern civilizations, an agent in the conflict in which the Eastern culture triumphed and made its first acquaintance with the magnificently beautiful tropical country which is situated 'far beyond the Pillars of Hercules.'"

As Frobenius sees it, this African Atlantis was the last fragmentary survival of a great prehellenic period in which the worship of Poseidon was the dominant force. Plato's story must be considered as an ensemble of memories relating to that period, for in his description of Atlantis is condensed the idea of a whole regional civilization which, starting from the Pacific, was slowly transmitted to Western Asia, then by the Mediterranean to the Atlantic seaboard, and finally over the Mediterranean southwards to Africa. In the course of its westward movement the particulars of this great emigrating civilization gradually altered, adapting themselves to each change of environment, but always preserving "the same spirit, in the same framework, appearing finally to be no less than a heritage." Each successive stage shows similarities which distinguish it from the surrounding remains of other ancient cultures and, allowing for differences due to localization, they are clearly connected. By a special cartographic method, which he himself evolved, Frobenius was able to show that the civilization of Yorubaland was specifically quite different from all other African cultures, and, in such particulars as its ruins, the shape of bows, tattooing, numerical symbolism, symbolic designs, oracles drawn from human sacrifices, and the respective sexes of the sun and moon in the Yoruba language, that it was connected with the civilizations localised in the central Pacific and linked to it by a chain of successive phases in Western Asia and along the Mediterranean. "Atlantean civilization is then an off-shoot of the solar period, a ray which has found its way across western Asia and the Mediterranean to Yorubaland and taken root. Atlantean culture is thus classified and catalogued as a whole and we have only to specify the details of these relations. Considered in this manner, Atlantic civilization is then in a sense an advance post of an evolution." Among many of these details Frobenius mentions the little bow of the Assyrians, and of the early Etruscan period, the use of metal plaques for a wall-covering as described in the Odyssey, and the sacred parasol of Kings, all of which, he says, have their characteristic diffusion in the Mediterranean region. He also gives a long list of the details which are concerned with the deeper spiritual side of the Yoruban civilization, and relates them with the ancient Kingdom of Benin, and the sacred city of the Yorubas, Ife, "where we have made archaeological discoveries of various stones, of terracottas, of copper moulds in the sacred places of this people, in their sacred woods and in their cemeteries. There too is the sacred grove where we found the bronze head of Olokon, in other words, the sea god Poseidon." Apparently the mythology of this god has no parallel in religious history except in the Etruscan doctrine of the thunderbolt. Frobenius also maintains that the prehellenic cult of Poseidon, carried by colonists from the East, found an isolated sanctuary at Tartessos, the Tarshish of the Bible, near the modern Cadiz. According to him the Tartesso-Etruscan civilization extended to West Africa, and the passage in *Kings I* (ch. 10, v. 22) "For the king had at sea a navy of Tarshish with the navy of Hiram; once in three years came the navy of Tarshish bringing gold, and silver, ivory, and apes, and peacocks," refers to the trade between the "gold coast" of Yorubaland and Tartessos. This identification rests upon his belief that the Uphaz from which, according to another Biblical passage (*Jeremiah* X, 9) associated with Tarshish, mariners brought gold, is really Yorubaland before the time of Benin; also that the Hebrew word translated "peacocks" ought to be emended to a very similar word in the Hebrew which would be translated "Ethiopian slaves."

(5)

Frobenius' work, to which it is impossible to do any sort of justice in a short space, is particularly interesting when considered in relation to the main Tartessian hypothesis, already mentioned in connection with the identification of Homer's Scheria. According to the exponents of this theory Atlantis and Scheria are both memories of Tartessos, the Biblical Tarshish, an ancient Bronze Age city at the mouth of the Guadalquivir. For Adolf Schulten, who first recognised in this region the resemblance to Plato's tradition of Atlantis the Biblical passage in which Ezekiel bewails the fall of Tyre (27, 12), has a special significance. "Tarshish was thy merchant by reason of the multitude of all kinds of riches; with silver, iron, tin and lead they traded in thy fairs." There was, he thinks, a town at Tartessos since very ancient times; first, perhaps, a Germanic settlement and, later, a Cretan colony with which the Tyrian Phoenicians traded. "The concordances between Atlantis and Tartessos are in fact so great that they cannot be fortuitous. Like Tartessos, the city of Atlantis is on an island near Gades (Cadiz), and is rich chiefly in metals, a very striking detail which applies to no other country as well as Tartessos. And among the metals which the Tartessian sailors imported zinc is mentioned and bronze which was an important industry among them." Hennig, who agrees with Schulten, says "everything that Plato reports of the paradisaic character of Atlantis seems an echo of old memories relating to Tartessos. Plato lived about the year

400. At this time the Greeks had thought of Tartessos
as a city which had been engulfed and disappeared no more
than 100 years ago. Certain souvenirs of this historical
Venice of the West could still have remained current at this
time." In this passage Schulten is referring to the sack of
Tartessos by the Carthaginians in 533 B.C. Another reason
why stories of cataclysm might have reached the East is
that in 509 B.C. the Carthaginians, who had since the sack
been masters of the city, made a treaty with Rome, by the
terms of which Carthaginians only had the right to navigate
outside the Pillars of Hercules; so that, as far as the
Mediterranean peoples living East of the straits were concerned, the straits were closed and Tartessos had "disappeared."

All this is excellent in theory, but it lacks the support
of archaeological evidence. The search for Tartessos-
Tarshish has not been a success and in 1926 Schulten had
to admit that Tartessos must be buried under the sea, for
he could find no trace of it at the mouth of Guadalquivir.
Three years later, however, Tartessos was once more in the
news when Mrs E. M. Wishaw published her *Atlantis in
Andalusia*, in which she claimed to have found evidence
of an extremely ancient Tartesso-Atlantean civilization
at Niebla, an ancient city on the Rio Tinto, a few miles
North-East of Huelva.

Mrs Wishaw, the directress of the Anglo-Spanish-Ameri-
can school of archaeology, had been studying the archaeology of Tartessos for twenty-five years when her book

appeared and her convictions have been treated with more
respect from the authorities than those of most advocates
of an Atlantean origin of Western civilization. "My theory,
to sum it up concisely, is that Plato's story is corroborated
from first to last by what we find here, even the Atlantean
name of his son Gadir who inherited that part of Poseidon's
kingdom beyond the Pillars of Hercules and ruled at Gades,
having its echo in the traditional Gadea on the Rio Tinto
in the jurisdiction of Niebla, an ancient mill under the
shadow of a Stone Age fortress, relics of which still stand."
Her conclusion, based on the evidence of neolithic exploita-
tion of the Rio Tinto mines and of skilled hydraulic
engineering at Niebla and Ronda in the dawn of the Copper
Age, is that Tartessos must be regarded as a colony of
Atlantis planted on the mainland from 12,000–40,000
years ago, and deriving its wealth from the export of Rio
Tinto minerals to the mother country. She cannot therefore be classified with Schulten and Hennig, who believe
that Atlantis *was* Tartessos and deny the existence of an
Atlantic island. Her theory must rather be considered as a
complementary to the work of Lewis Spence, whose main
hypothesis, which she accepts, will be reserved for detailed
consideration later on.

(6)

Another well-argued case recently summed up by its
author is that of Dr F. Gidon, who maintains that Plato's
Atlantis contains an echo of the land subsidences between

Brittany and Ireland which opened up the English Channel. His case is primarily botanical.

The theory rests upon the author's claim to have shown that the humid climate of the new post-glacial period (favourable to the spread of forests) which succeeded the old dry post-glacial period (favourable to steppe grasses) did not establish itself till the Bronze Age, *i.e.* 2,500 years before our era; and that this climatic change was established as the result of the submergences on the west and north west coasts of France and on the site of the English Channel. This period, historical in Egypt, was still prehistoric in Northern Europe; but commercial relations between Northern and Southern Europe had long existed. "Could not the Atlantean legend as Plato has transmitted it to us have originated in the more or less vague knowledge, which must have existed in Southern Europe, of the submergences which had taken place in the north? That is the question which I have been asking since 1914–15. Atlantean civilization, as Plato described it, is, in fact, a Bronze Age civilization."

In 1914 Gidon's dating of the submergences differed from the general opinion which placed them in the last part of the Tertiary period, *i.e.* before the Ice Age. This opinion, he points out, was the chief reason for the summary dismissal by geologists of the Atlantic theories of Atlantis; but since 1923 botanists have been inclined to place the Atlantic submergences much later in order to explain the distribution of certain species, and they have since admitted that "lands or close chains of islands did still join Ireland to great Britain during the Ice Age, and probably also to the Iberian Peninsula and the Azores, allowing flora and fauna to be communicated." It has also been argued that the English Channel could only have been opened up in the Bronze Age, since certain vegetable species travelling from east to west *via* Germany before the Bronze Age were able to cross over to England, whereas others, arriving later, were stopped by the sea and unable to cross.

The dating of the end of the old glacial climate and of the Atlantic submergences in the bronze age can be further determined by traces of the residual flora of the old cold climate in neolithic mounds in Normandy. Gidon's argument, very much condensed, is roughly as follows. It is known that the residual cold temperature flora have made no headway since the change of climate, and that they are also incapable of surviving the shortest period of forest invasion. Botanists think therefore that the areas in which they are found have never been forested and that the presence of such flora in any soil substratum indicates that this substratum must also have been there since before the change of climate. Hence, the discovery of flora of the cold period in the neolithic mound at Condé-sur-Ifs in Normandy proves the mound to have been constructed before the change of climate, *i.e.* that the climate had not yet changed in the New Stone Age, which immediately preceded the Bronze Age.

The extent and area of the submerged lands can also be

gauged. The extent is shown by the fact that at the time when the neolithic tumulus at Conde-sur-Ifs was constructed, the climate of Basse-Normandy was more continental (*i.e.* less influenced by the sea) than the *present* climate of La Champagne; and therefore the area of the land which prevented maritime influences being felt in Normandy was "at least as wide as modern France from La Champagne to the ocean." As to the situation of the submerged lands, it has been shown that certain particularly continental elements of the former cold-temperature in Normandy are lacking in the corresponding species in the west, which means that the original climate of the west was much less continental than that of the north and that the old coast line was much nearer the west than the north.

"From the above observations we may conclude," says Gidon, "that the lands which disappeared in the Bronze Age were situated more to the north-west of France than to the west and that their extent in a north-westerly direction corresponds at least to the breadth of modern France; which suggests a location, first on the site of the present channel, then on the site of the coast, now submerged, which joined the extremity of Great Britain to Ireland and in the middle of which was the old mouth of the Seine. In other words these lands correspond exactly to the great submerged plateau whose limits are defined on the charts by the line of 200 metre soundings, outside which the depth of the sea rapidly increases."

Gidon, however, does not attempt to ascribe the whole

of the Platonian tradition of Atlantis to the Ireland-Brittany submergences. He concludes rather that the Atlantean folklore known to Plato derived from several sources, of which the Northern submergences was only one. But he points out that there are certain elements of the Atlantis legend which can be explained by supposing a northern source.

(1) The "sea-rams" of which Ælien speaks (See Appendix C) in connection with Atlantis were probably seals. The fact that they are described as "wintering" in Corsica shows them to be strange to the southern climate of the Mediterranean.

(2) Plato's description of Atlantis as "outside the Pillars of Hercules " may mean "in the northern sea." The old geographers confused the west and north-west of Europe to such an extent that Strabo orientates the Pyrenees not east and west but north and south.

(3) Although the climate of Plato's island seems on the whole to be hot and in some ways tropical, in other places it seems to be temperate with a winter season more pronounced than the present winter in Madeira and the Canaries. Plato speaks of baths different for winter and summer and recommends a certain part of the island as sheltered from the north wind.

The lands situated between Brittany and Ireland in the Bronze Age would have had a humid ocean climate, especially on the gulf open to the south west, and this fits in with Plato's description.

(4) The lands submerged in the Bronze Age at the entrance of the channel were situated eaxctly between the region of England where the Romans later mined their tin and the ancient zinc and copper mines found in Brittany and the Vendée. Atlantis according to Plato was exceedingly rich in metals.

(5) A number of Greek historians speak of Celts or Cimbri and other peoples as living in a state of perpetual recoil from advancing seas, in some cases migrating to other lands. Poseidonius, in particular, says that the Cimbri, dislodged by inundations, emigrated and crossed the whole of Europe as far as the sea of Azov, *i.e.* from west to east. Now it is to be noted that the submergences which actually happened in the Bronze Age also progressed from west to east. "It therefore seems possible that Atlantes was the first name for the people (known by Atlantic sea route) whose territory was in the extreme west of Europe between Ireland and Brittany and who were obliged to emigrate in the Bronze Age (still a legendary period). The name Celts or Cimbri was subsequently applied to these people (known by the continental route) whose territory, situated more in the east (Channel, North Sea, Baltic), was not submerged till later, in the by-then historical periods of the end of the Bronze Age or the Iron Age."

Gidon also considers that Plato's account of the swiftness of the cataclysm which overtook the Atlanteans is quite probable. He recalls that in this very region the whole of the Zuyder Zee was submerged in one day (1282).

(6) Is Plato the sole author to know of an Atlantic civilization outside the Pillars of Hercules? Gidon thinks that the Celts known to Ephorus (a contemporary of Plato) were either the same as Plato's Atlanteans or their direct descendants and that the reason they are not called by the same name is that information concerning them came by another route. According to Strabo the name of Celts was applied to all the peoples of the north as far as the Atlantic, so that the peoples whe were migrating east as the northern land subsidences took place would also come under this name. If this be so, the Celtic migrations may be represented in Plato by the warlike campaigns of the Atlanteans upon the mainland. According to Plato the Atlanteans had founded establishments on the north of the Mediterranean basin as far as Etruria. Poseidonius says that the Cimbri, starting from the North Sea, penetrated as far as the Black Sea. Their Atlantic predecessors then migrating from the channel region in the Bronze Age could also have penetrated as far as Etruria.

The probability is that at first the peoples who were being driven back from the western seaboard followed the old course of the Tertiary Seine as far as Scandinavia, where, according to modern theories, they may have become the first Germans. This conclusion is suggested by a special technique in preparing marine salt, which is peculiar only to Normandy and the coast of Jutland and points to a possible trace of these early migrations.

(7)

In opposition to all of the foregoing theories of Atlantis in the west and north is the work of the orientalist Karst. His conception of Atlantis is founded upon the old cosmological conception of an eastern and a western Ethiopia, an island of the sun both in the east and west, and Pillars of Hercules to east and west. Karst believes that there were also two islands of Atlantis.

The complete theory is summed up for the first time in untechnical language by Alexander Bessmertny.

"Karst shows that there was an early Atlantis by the Indo-Persian ocean, and also another western, Libyan and Hesperidean Atlantis in North Africa, which at that time was still linked to Italy by a Sicilian-Tunisian land-bridge, in the shape of a peninsula."

"The original Atlantis of the Indo-Persian ocean is the country of the Ibero-Ethiopian peoples. These peoples constituted the great race which should be considered as the first vehicle of civilization; to this group belong the Sumerians and Elamites, the civilised pre-Aryan people of the early Indies, the pre-Hamitic proto-Egyptians, the Turditano-Iberians of Spain and a primitive cultivated people called the Ibero-Atlantic Celts. Karst identified the Greek island of Ogygia with this early Atlantis (see Plutarch. Appendix C.); it was also identified with the South Ethiopian lands of the Indo-Arabian sea. This early land of Ogygia-Atlantis must be imagined as an antediluvian island-continent, almost as a continuation of the

south east coast of Arabia, stretching towards Madagascar
and Ceylon: it disappeared at the beginning of the Ice Age
at the time of the Ogygian deluge of Pelasgian tradition.
Karst sees in this catastrophe the cause of the Atlantean
migration. The central point of his Atlantean theory is the
conviction that at the time when the north of Europe
was mostly under ice, the pre-Hamitic Ibero-Ethiopians,
as colonists and civilisers of the Libyan South-Mediter-
ranean zone, spread, pushing out from the Indian ocean,
over Iran and South-west Asia, over the country of the
upper Nile, transversely across the North African sea
coast which was then covered with lagoons, towards
Numidia, Mauretania, Hisperia; and thence, over western
Spain, towards the sea-coast of Gaul and Britain, covering
this region everywhere with dolmens and megaliths as
witnesses to their civilization and religion. Karst thus
speaks of the Indo-Atlantic race of dolmen builders.

"Very remarkable is his observation that according to
the earliest language-forms the Atlantic sea was considered
as double, with an eastern basin and a western basin. In
its original sense the conception of Libya and Ethiopia
was applied to countries in south-western Asia, in touch
with the Indo-Arabian ocean; but this sense gradually
fell into disuse and the words, losing their locality value,
became applied to the African territory in the other
Atlantic basin. For Strabo the South Asiatic sea is still
an 'atlantic' sea which he supposes to be joined to the
western Atlantic sea. . . .

"There was also according to Karst a second western Atlantis in Libya and the Hesperides, constituted by 'Africa Minor,' stretching from Tunis to Morocco and peninsular in form. This region was then attached to Italy by a Sicilian-Tunisian land-bridge, while to the south and east it was cut off like an island by the sea which covered the Sahara. Karst thinks that this land was a continuation of an archipelago which later disappeared; the Cape Verde Islands, the Canaries and the Azores are the remnants.

"This western Atlantis must also have been destroyed in a great flood and Karst believes that in Plato's account reports of the sinking of both Atlantic Islands were already confused, because even the Egyptian source from which Plato's story came by then no longer differentiated between the two cataclysms."

Karst's hypothesis is built up on elaborate ethnological and linguistic considerations, better left untouched than inadequately summarized; but it is of special importance on view of the prevailing opinion among ethnologists that civilization came originally from the east. It is also important because it shows the danger of drawing facile conclusions from the extraordinarily complicated tangle of racial migrations, racial mixtures, and racial influences in which the origin of peoples and the true sense of ancient history lies hidden. Its secondary use is to act as a large pinch of strong and coarse salt to be taken with the other theories of Atlantis, to steel the mind against the appeal of more ingenuity such, for instance, as Hermann's conception of the proper scale of the Atlantis which he fits so neatly into Tunisia.

(8)

Reviewing the hypotheses we have so far sketched[6] certain general criticisms come to mind. Those which depend on the results of archaeological fieldwork (Tartessos, Tunisia, Morocco) have not yet produced sufficient body of evidence to be more than suggestive, let alone to have proved their case. Tartessos, like Atlantis, has been attributed to many parts of the globe, and to find the two identified, looks like a simplification of convenience rather than necessity. Birds of a feather snared together . . . All Atlantean protagonists, except Gidon, who recognises that Plato's tradition must have been drawn from several sources, and Karst who recognizes a confusion of two sources, tend to an uncritically fundamental belief in the *details* of Plato's text, while rejecting the *framework*, an island situated outside the Pillars of Hercules destroyed in an ocean cataclysm. Plato got his geography wrong, say the Tunisians, the Moroccans and, more politely, the Tartessians and Frobenius, and all are agreed that his dating of the catastrophe is absurd. Plato was wrong, too, about Atlantis being an island. It was a land-bridge, part of the mainland, a peninsula; some say that it must have been overwhelmed by the sea, others that it was not submerged at all but buried in sand. Yet in the case of the topographical and architectural details of the Atlantean citadel (that part of the story for which a study of the texts gives us most reason to hold Plato's "invention" responsible) they take the greatest trouble to establish a comparison. To the present writer it seems clear that all who start by rejecting Plato's data about the position, status and fate of Atlantis are lacking in critical appreciation of the Platonic dialogues. Nevertheless there may be some truth in all of them, and it is obviously safer to try and reconcile conflicting theories, where possible, than to reject them out of hand.

There remains the chief hypothesis ; Atlantis as an island in the Atlantic ocean. Oddly enough this interpretation, which is the natural one, has received less attention than the others and it is only in recent years that it has been seriously reconsidered. But it is not difficult to find a present justification for singling it out for fuller consideration than the rest.

Regarded as a scientific proof of the existence of an Atlantic island traditionally remembered as Plato's Atlantis it gets us no further than any of the others. It is an hypothesis, no more. But at least it is an honest attempt to face the explicit meaning of Plato's text despite the warnings of the geologists and ethnologists. Also it is the only scientific theory tolerable from the romantic point of view; and this, it has already been suggested, is essential in determining the *value* of Atlantis. If, in the present state of stalemate, it is worth trying at all to show that the symbolic tragedy in Plato's story bears any relation to fact, surely the one essential of that story which *requires* a historical foundation is that of an island continent peopled by human descendants of Poseidon and separated from the rest of the prehistoric world by an ocean subservient to hostile gods. For those who feel the poetic justness of this theme, no theory which supposes Atlantis to be a submerged continental appendage or as an inland city buried beneath the desert sand, can fail to produce a sense of disappointment that the possible or probable truth should fall so far short of Plato's account; it would be better, like Jowett, to count Atlantis "a noble lie" rather than see it related to facts so unworthy of the fiction. Either Atlantis is an island in the Atlantic ocean or it is not "Atlantis" at all.

(9)

The theory that Atlantis was really, as Plato says, an island in the Atlantic ocean was first presented by a Frenchman, Cadet, in 1787. According to him the Azores and the Canaries were the remains of it. Bory de St. Vincent supported this view in his *"Essaie sur les isles fortunées et l'antique Atlantide."* But the theory did not become popular until the publication in 1882 of Ignatius Donelly's *Antediluvian World*.

According to Donelly, Atlantis was the original home of nearly all the arts and sciences and the fount of all civilization. In his famous last chapter, the reconstruction of

137

Atlantis, he credits this "great, wise, and civilized race" with having known, amongst other things, gunpowder and the use of the magnet; their religious worship was simple and pure; they had attained to the conception of "one universal, omnipotent, great First Cause"; they were also the inventors of medical science and among their achievements in this sphere was the practice of circumcision to stamp out the ravages of syphilis!

The effect of Donelly's book was tremendous, It was translated into many languages and is still for many people the be-all and end-all of Atlantean studies. His theory, partly developed from the work of another American, Hosea, was based on the resemblances between the ancient civilizations of the old and new worlds. The presence of obelisks, sphinxes, pyramids and cults of the dead in both continents was for him a proof of their common cultural origin in the Atlantic; and having postulated this common origin he declared that the analogous civilizations of Egypt and Mexico in ancient times must have been colonies of Atlantis.

The propositions which he set out to demonstrate have had such a lasting effect among the Atlantis-minded that it is worth quoting them in full.

i. "That there once existed in the Atlantic ocean, opposite the mouth of the Mediterranean sea, a large island, which was the remnant of an Atlantic continent, and known to the ancient world as Atlantis."

ii. "That the description of this island given by Plato

is not as has been long supposed, fable, but veritable history."

iii. "That Atlantis was the region where man first rose from a state of barbarism to civilization."

iv. "That it became in the course of ages a populous and mighty nation, from whose overflowings the shores of the gulf of Mexico, the Mississippi River, the Amazon, the Pacific coast of South America, the Mediterranean, the west coast of Africa and Europe, the Baltic, the Black Sea, and the Caspian were populated by civilized nations."

v. "That it was the true antediluvian world; the Garden of Eden, the Gardens of the Hesperides; the Elysian Fields; the Gardens of Alcinous; the Mesompholus; the Olympus; the Asgard of the traditions of the ancient nations; representing a universal memory of a great land, where early mankind dwelt for ages in peace and happiness."

vi. "That the gods and goddesses of the ancient Greeks, the Hindus, the Phoenicians, and the Scandinavians were simply the kings, queens and heroes of Atlantis; and the acts attributed to them in mythology are a confused recollection of real historical events."

vii. "That the mythology of Egypt and Peru represented the original religion of Atlantis, which was sun-worship."

viii. "That the oldest colony formed by the Atlanteans was probably in Egypt, whose civilization was a reproduction of that of the Atlantic island."

ix. "That the implements of the 'Bronze Age' of

139

Europe were derived from Atlantis. The Atlanteans were also the first manufacturers of Iron."

x. "That the Phoenician alphabet, parent of all the European alphabets, was derived from an Atlantis alphabet, which was also conveyed from Atlantis to the Mayas of Central America."

xi. "That Atlantis was the original seat of the Aryan or Indo-European family of nations, as well as of the Semitic peoples, and possibly also of the Turanian races."

xii. "That Atlantis perished in a terrible convulsion of nature, in which the whole island was sunk in the sea, with nearly all its inhabitants."

xiii. "That a few persons escaped in ships and on rafts, and carried to the nations east and west the tidings of the appalling catastrophe, which has survived to our own time in the Flood and Deluge legends of the different nations of the old and new worlds."

(10)

In 1924 Lewis Spence, the Scottish mythologist, published his *Problem of Atlantis*. It was obvious from the preface that here at least was a book which required serious consideration. The purpose of it was "not so much to demonstrate the former existence of an Atlantean continent as to place the study of the whole problem on a more accurate basis than has yet been attempted in modern times." Later, his theory was fully developed in *Atlantis in America* (1925) and *The history of Atlantis* (1928).

It is significant that Lewis Spence does not, like his predecessors, attempt to uphold the untenable theory that Atlantis flourished as late as the Bronze Age. He is prepared to admit that Atlantis did not know the use of metals but denies that metals are necessary to a high culture, insisting that Atlantis, if it existed as an island in the Atlantic ocean, must have been a Stone Age civilization. He also removes what was one of the worst flaws of Donelly's argument by attempting to explain the disparity between the relative dates of the ancient civilizations of the old and new worlds. If the Mayas and the Egyptians really had a common origin in the Atlantis it is very strange that whereas the civilization of ancient Egypt can be dated back as early as the 4th millenium B.C., the earliest traces of civilization in America cannot be traced back earlier than three centuries before the Christian era. He also rejects as fantastic the notion that Atlantis was the mother of all civilization. To infer from the obvious fact that civilization must have started somewhere that the entire apparatus of civilization was derived from any single source is unscientific, for it is equally obvious that many of the special and separate manifestations of civilization are due to environment.

Geologically speaking Spence sets out to prove the following propositions.[7]

i.   "That a great continent formerly occupied the whole or major portion fo the North Atlantic region, and a considerable portion of its southern basin. Of early geological origin, it must, in the course of successive ages, have experienced many changes in contour and mass, probably undergoing frequent submergence and emergence."

ii. "That in Miocene (late Tertiary) times it still retained its continental character, but towards the end of that period it began to disintegrate, owing to successive volcanic and other causes."

iii. "That this disintegration resulted in the formation of greater and lesser insular masses. Two of these, considerably larger in area than any of the others, were situated (*a*) at a relatively short distance from the entrance to the Mediterranean and (*b*) in the region of the present West India Islands. These may be respectively called Atlantis and Antillia. Communication was possible between them by an insular chain."

iv. "That these two island-continents and the connecting chain of islands persisted until late Pleistocene times, at which epoch (about 25,000 years ago, or the beginning of the Post-Glacial epoch) Atlantis seems to have experienced further disintegration. Final disaster seems to have overtaken Atlantis about 10,000 B.C. Antillia, on the other hand, seems to have survived until a much more recent period, and still persists fragmentarily in the Antillean (Antilles) group, or the West India Islands.

"It would seem then that if Atlantean culture reached America it must have done so by way of the Antillian continent."

Through a Glass Darkly

(11)

As a general introduction to the whole theory Spence lays special emphasis upon the power and persistence of the Atlantean legend. "Just as a great world intuition regarding a transatlantic continent prevailed in the time of Columbus, so a similar instinct, overwhelming and ineradicable, is being manifested in our day regarding the existence of a great continent in the Atlantic Ocean in times past. This belief unquestionably has its origin in folk-memory, and is thus safe from the assaults of that description of science which has ever held tradition in disesteem."

In examining the dialogues of Plato he states his belief, chiefly on internal grounds, in the "substantial and general accuracy and historicity" of that account; but he is by no means a fundamentalist and he does not accept Plato's statement about prehistoric Athens being mixed up with the Atlanteans; he says that the account of the war between Athens and Atlantis is probably a memory of a foreign defeat in the Aegean at some early date. Another conclusion drawn from Plato's account is that ancient Carthage, a recent reconstruction of which seemed closely to resemble the citadel of Atlantis, must have been planned in accordance with an ancient Atlantean design long in vogue in North West Africa and Western Europe. The descriptions of the metals in the *Critias* are *a priori* unhistorical, since it is geologically impossible for Atlantis to have sunk later than 9,600 B.C., *i.e.* in the New Stone Age, 6,000 years before metals came into use; but he quotes M. Termier,

143

of the Geological Survey of France, in support of the possible existence of the white, black and red stones on the site of the sunk Atlantis.

The main pillar of Spence's hypothesis is the geological evidence for the existence and survival of an Atlantic continent till a period sufficiently late to be contemporaneous with *homo sapiens* capable of transmitting the tradition of it. "If then," says Spence, "we are to search for a lost Atlantis peopled by types recognizable as modern, or semi-civilized, the period in which we must do so is narrowed down to Post-Glacial time—that is, to the last 25,000 years of European history. What has geology to tell us of the probability of the existence of such a continent during this period? *We must remember that it is not by any means incumbent upon us to attempt to justify Plato's account word for word. That is the grand error that has been made by nearly every one of our predecessors in this quest. It is obvious that we are dealing with a great world-memory, of which Plato's story is merely one of the broken and distorted fragments, and we must seek to justify its broad contentions not by reference to any solitary and possibly fallible account, but by all other reasonable means as well.*"

He then quotes the opinions of a number of geologists of standing. All, he says, are now agreed that there was once a land-bridge between the old and new worlds. But M. Termier believes the ocean to be a great volcanic zone, the eastern part of which is still unstable and concludes that a great deal of it was only submerged quite recently.

This conclusion is based on the mountainous character of the ocean bed in the region of the Azores, the volcanic nature of the islands in the ocean depression West of the African-European zone, and the fact that the lava and other volcanic detritus which has been brought up from the ocean bed north of the Azores between Cape Cod and Brest must have cooled quite recently under atmospheric pressure, *i.e.* above water. According to Termier the Platonian history of the Atlantic is highly probable. Professor Scharff of Dublin also indicates the volcanic nature of the Atlantic islands and states his belief that up to Tertiary times the Azores and Madeira were connected with Portugal; there was in his opinion a south Atlantic continent as well stretching from Morocco and the Canaries southwards towards South America. The northern part remained until Miocene (late Tertiary) times when the Azores and Madeira became isolated from Europe and the north and south Atlantic became joined. More recently Scharff stated his belief that the Atlantic islands were reunited with the Old World in the early part of the Ice Age when man, who had already appeared in western Europe, could have reached these islands by land. Professor Gregory thinks that the Atlantic islands are fragments of an Atlantic continent into which the Atlas and Alpine ranges were once produced; and Professor Hull characterises the Azores as peaks of a submerged continent which flourished in the Ice Age. On zoological and botanical grounds Hull also supports the theory that there was a common centre

145

in the Atlantic where life began. He states that after a careful study of the admiralty charts he has come to the conclusion that at the time when the Atlantean continent existed there was another western or Antillean continent shutting off the Caribbean Sea and the Gulf of Mexico from the Gulf Stream.

As to the existence of this Antillean continent Spence says that the concensus of geological opinion supports it, but admits that in the general view it was partially submerged in Tertiary times, rising afterwards to its present position as an archipelago, consisting of the Lesser and Greater Antilles.

He quotes, however, a number of geologists whose opinions seem to him to support his contention that the Antillean continent survived till a "relatively late period."

The geological case for an original Tertiary Atlantean–Antillean continent is supplemented by evidence from the distribution of animal and plant life which, according to various testimonies, proves a land connection between Europe, Africa and America. The presence of rabbits in the Azores since a time previous to the official discovery of the islands; the existence of 65 species of burrowing beetles, called Amphisbonidae,[8] distributed only in America, Africa and the Mediterranean region; the fact that identical forms of earthworm are found exclusively in North Africa, Europe and the Atlantic islands; and the marked affinity between forms of a crustacean called the Freshwater Decapod on both sides of the Atlantic, are among the points cited by Scharff as conclusive evidence in favour of the existence of a former land connection between Africa and South America, and between Europe and the Atlantic Isles.

M. Germain, who has also studied the fauna of the Atlantic Isles, agrees that their origin was continental. He states that the Pulmonata Mollusca called Oleacinidae are peculiar only to Central America, the West Indies, the Mediterranean basin and the Atlantic Isles; and that this distribution implies the extension of the Atlantic continent at the beginning of Miocene times to the West Indies, but he thinks that the continent was separated from the West Indies towards the close of the Miocene period. M. Termier, commenting on M. Germain's deductions, says that they can only be explained "by the persistence up to very nearly the present times of a maritime shore extending from the West Indies to Senegal, and even binding together Florida, the Bermudas and the bottom of the Gulf of Guinea."

However, as Spence himself admits, most of this life dates from the Tertiary period, so that evidence as to its distribution does not greatly assist the argument for an Atlantic continent in Late Quaternary times. But it shows at least that the continent was not yet submerged in Tertiary times.

He also mentions two other details, which, though they cannot be classified as strictly biological evidence, are extremely dramatic.

"More than one acute observer of animal life has made allusion to a strange and fatal habit of the lemmings of Norway. The lemming, a small rodent, occasionally receives a migratory instinct which sends it southward in great numbers. Most of these animals annually leave the Norwegian coast, and swim out far into the Atlantic. On reaching the spot to which the migratory instinct has so unerringly called them, they circle round for some considerable time, as if in search of land, but, failing in their quest, gradually sink exhausted into the depths. Similarly it is well known that large flocks of birds annually fly to a part of the Atlantic where no land is now visible, and after fluttering about in dismay for some considerable time, fall exhausted into the water."

(12)

Having established that there *is* a geological case for the survival of such an island as Plato's Atlantis until a period compatible with the existence of man, Spence then proceeds to examine the evidence from prehistoric times. Do we know of any type of prehistoric man living early enough to have come from Atlantis, yet sufficiently civilized to have been capable of transmitting the tradition of the cataclysm which destroyed it?

We do in fact know of such a people. At the close of the post-glacial part of the Ice Age (25,000 years ago) a race of palaeolithic (early Stone Age) men arrived in the region of the Bay of Biscay supplanting the low, apelike

Neanderthal man who had hitherto sparsely inhabited the continent. These newcomers were comparatively highly civilized[9] and judging from the skull measurements of the available specimens their average brain content was greater than that of modern man. They were tall and broad-shouldered; their arms were short in comparison to their legs (an indication of high racial development); they had high cheek-bones, thin noses and massive chins. According to Sir Arthur Keith they were mentally and physically one of the finest races the world has ever seen.

These Cro-Magnons (the name comes from the place in S.W. France where their relics were first discovered) were cave-dwellers and probably wore skins to protect them from the intense cold. Their tools, which were of flint, bone and horn, were vastly superior in variety and technique to those of the Neanderthals who had used only very rudimentary flints. Their skill and inventiveness is particularly apparent from the implements they fashioned for fishing. Such burial places as have been found are full of flints, pebbles, perforated shells, teeth and other objects which were probably charms and amulets; in some cases traces of red paint have been found on bones implying that red paint or ochre had been rubbed on the body after death to give it the appearance of continued life and health, a sympathetic-magical practice by which it was hoped that the corpse's health in another sphere would be insured. The Cro-Magnons also had a comparatively highly developed art and many of their stone engravings and rock

149

paintings are of such a high order that they suggest a culture which must already have existed for many thousands of years in some other part of the world. The subjects depicted are mostly animals, bears, mammoths, horses, deer, and occasional bas-reliefs of the human form. Cro-Magnon art (generally known as Aurignacian from the station found at Aurignac in S. France) is common to stations along the Biscayan coasts of France and Spain. There are also Aurignacian stations along the Mediterranean coast, in the South of France, in Sicily, North Africa and in the Italian and Iberian peninsulas.

The culture distribution is extremely wide and authorities are divided as to where it originated; but an eastern origin is improbable since its earlier stages have not yet been met with in eastern and central Europe. A northern origin is even more unlikely. But there is no doubt about the existence of early Aurignacian culture forms in Africa; the question then boils down to a choice between North Africa and the Pyrenean-Biscayan region. Spence says that they came from the north-west, since the earliest pure Aurignacian has been found in the Biscay region;, but Professor J. L. Myres, writing in the *Cambridge Ancient History*, thinks that the Cro-Magnons came from Africa. Even so, says Spence, that does not upset the Atlantean hypothesis "which regards an African or Biscayan secondary origin for Aurignacian culture with equal placidity." For him the most important opinion is that of the Abbé Breuil who considers that successive waves of culture came either from the south or Mediterranean region, or from the Atlantic or Biscayan zone.

Two other reasons are given for looking west for the original home of the Cro-Magnons. First, there is the theory advanced by the French anthropologist Dr Verneau, Lord Abercromby, and, rather tentatively, by Professor Osborne, that there is a racial relation between the Cro-Magnons and the aboriginal Guanches of the Canary islands; from which Spence concludes that the Guanche-Cro-Magnon was a survival of the Atlantean race, as the Canaries were a survival of the Atlantean continent. Secondly, he quotes Osborne in rather timid support of Ripley's theory that the Basque peoples of the Pyrenees speak a language derived from the Cro-Magnons. "This hypothesis is well worth considering, for it is not inconceivable that the ancestors of the Basques conquered the Cro-Magnons and subsequently acquired their language." Now it is significant that the Basque tongue has no linguistic affinities with any other European language, on the contrary, according to Dr Farrer's families of speech, it strongly resembles in its grammatical structure the aboriginal languages of America, and those alone.

After many thousands of years the civilization of Western Europe underwent a "technical invasion," and there begins a new period known to the anthropologists as the Magdelanian or Capsian. This new culture which, like its predecessor, rose from an unknown source about 16,000 years ago, is considered to be a new phase of Cro-Magnon or Aurignacian civilization refreshed by the Solutrean smooth flint culture and a much better technique of art and tool making. It is a renaissance, but, says Breuil, "it appears as if the fundamental elements of the superior Aurignacian culture had been contributed by *some unknown route* to constitute the kernel of the Magdalenian civilization while the Solutrean episode was going on elsewhere." Spence comments: "This can only mean that the older Aurignacian art received impetus and stimulation from its original and parent source"—Atlantis. The proof for him lies in the fact that Solutrean flint culture, which came originally from Libya or Somaliland, never reached as far as the southern Pyrenees and the Cro-Magnons south of that barrier were not affected by it; hence it must have been of extraneous origin.

10,000 years ago there was a third "invasion " by people known as the Azilians (from the Mas D'Azil cave in Spain) and "once again we have to look to the Pyrenees and Biscay for the first traces of a people arriving at a period long before that in which European history begins." Their handling of flints and bones was brought to a high pitch of smoothness and delicacy. They had a high geometric art and seem to have reduced their paintings to a kind of symbolism which suggests the beginning of the writing idea. The men wore feather headdresses and short trousers, the women short skirts and caps, and were covered with ornaments. Azilian culture is also found in its earliest stages in North Africa and South-west Europe, and the

Abbé Breuil believes that it came from circum-Mediterranean sources; but there is no concensus of opinion about their origin, which remains vague. Several facts, however, seem to Spence to point to a western origin.

1. They were invariably buried with their faces towards the west.

2. They were a seafaring race. Where did they learn the art of navigation? Mackenzie believes they learnt it in Egypt on the calm waters of the Nile, but no data exists to show that the Egyptians sailed the sea before 5,000 B.C. The Azilian flint fishhooks are too big to have been used for anything except deep sea fishing; and authorities have called them "a population of fishermen." This, in conjunction with the fact that there are many stations in Biscay, suggests that they originated by the ocean; but though they were a maritime race it is not necessary to suppose that they reached Europe by sea, since they probably reached Africa, and later, Europe, by a land-bridge, or by a closely knit insular chain.

3. The date of their arrival in Europe corresponds with the date given by Plato for the sinking of Atlantis.

(13)

These Azilians, Spence argues, were the parents of the Iberians and to this fact we are to attribute the wide diffusion of legends of cataclysm in those countries which were inhabited by an original Iberian stock. Azilian "colonists" founded the civilizations of Egypt and Crete.

Though it cannot be denied that the beginnings of modern European civilization came from Egypt, the probability is that it was only returning in the direction from which it originally came, the West.

At this point Mrs Wishaw's evidence about the neolithic Tartessian-Iberian civilization of Andalusia lends considerable weight to the somewhat bare ethnological argument of Spence. It shows, too, the common ground between superficially irreconcilable theories of Atlantis in North Africa (Berlioux, Prorok, etc), Atlantis as Tartessos (Schulten and Hennig), and Atlantis as an Atlantic island. Mrs Wishaw differs from Spence only in her belief that Atlantis was still above the water in the Copper Age of the Rio Tinto district—*i.e.* in neolithic times. Among the archaeological proofs for the great antiquity and high civilization of the race who built the fortress, hydraulic works and inland harbour at Niebla as well as the sun-temple at Seville she cites the discovery in a neolithic cave of a beautifully worked file and cascobel of copper. She considers this cave to be a prehistoric mining-shaft, 8,000–10,000 years old.

As further evidence that the Tartessian civilization could not have been founded, as is generally supposed, by the Phoenicians between 900 and 800 B.C. she shows that no less than 147 Iberian alphabetic signs, collected by her in Andalusia, are duplicated in the prehistoric rock-paintings of Libya; and this supports her contention that there was a common Libya-Tartessian culture springing originally from Atlantis. "I hold," she writes, "that the marvellously civilised prehistoric people whose civilization I have put on record sprang from the fusion of the prehistoric Libyans, with the Atlantes, later to be known as Libyans, who in an earlier stage of the history of humanity came to Andalusia from Atlantis to purchase the gold, silver and copper provided by the neolithic miners of Rio Tinto, and in the course of generations of friendly intercourse, welded the Iberian and African cultures so closely together that eventually Tartessos and Africa had a race in common, which was the Liby-Tartessian."

Some of Mrs Wishaw's proofs of the Libyan penetration into Iberian Spain in prehistoric times are extremely interesting. In a neolithic sepulchral cave, known as the Cave of the Bats, in the province of Granada, 12 skeletons were discovered, sitting in a circle round a central skeleton of a woman, dressed in a leather tunic. At the entrance of the cave were three more skeletons, one wearing a crown and dressed in a tunic of finely woven esparto grass. Beside the skeletons were hide bags containing carbonised food, and other bags were filled with poppy heads, flowers and amulets; poppy heads were scattered all over the floor of the cave. Among a number of other objects were some little clay discs similar to discs identified by archaeologists as necklace ornaments connected with the sun-cult, found in the land harbour at Niebla and in a building trench near Seville.

The explanation given by the Spanish archaeologist Sr. de Gongora is that the skeletons were a royal family of Iberians who, when hard pressed in battle by invading tribes, decided to be walled up in the cave to die rather than risk capture. The crowned figure was, of course, the king; the woman in the centre of the ring of skeletons, an Amazon princess of the royal house, probably the wife or daughter of the chief. They had committed suicide by eating poppy opium, a method known in Roman times and possibly learnt from Iberians during the Roman occupation. That they had been walled up of their own free will, to die and not merely to take refuge, was indicated by the size of the boulders which sealed the mouth of the cave and by the discovery not far away from the entrance, of a monolith which was probably erected by their tribesmen to commemorate them.

This data must be considered in relation to a neolithic cup, found near Seville, which depicts a native Iberian Amazon dressed exactly like the woman in the Cave of the Bats, in the last throes of a death-struggle with two Libyan chieftains. The chieftains are shown to be Libyan by their helmet plumes and kilts, their side tresses and the murderous looking double-headed axes, later recorded as in use among the Libyans of the Carthaginian army.

Mrs Wishaw produces a mass of evidence from a comparison of the manners, culture and religion of Tartessians and Libyans to support her theory of a common origin in the west. Among the survivals of the Liby-Tartessian sun-cult is an ancient sun temple lying 6½ metres

below the Calle Abades in Seville. It is a strange labyrinthine structure with one sensational feature—a circular
tomb sealed by a great monolith, with a roof so delicately
vaulted and ribbed that there can be no doubt that it was
meant to represent the sun's rays pouring in from the sky.
A corresponding chapel-vault on the other side of the
building is walled up with material precisely similar to that
of the prehistoric chambers of the Queen's tower at Niebla,
which dates the temple as certainly neolithic, if not earlier.
Here, beneath the streets of the city of Seville, according to
Mrs Wishaw, lies the remnant of the lost capital of
Tartessos, Tarshish.

A further link between ancient Tartessos and Libya can
be found in the study of the primitive matriarchate in the
earlier stages of Libyan society, which still survives in the
not uncommon North African custom of the mother being
the head of the family; its survival in Graeco-Roman times
would account for Diodorus Siculus's story of the Amazons
which, as we have seen, was the basis of Berlioux's theory
of the Atlantean origin of the Berber tribes; but Mrs
Wishaw deduces from her observation of present-day
manners and customs in Spain and from some prehistoric
ex-voto statuettes found round Seville, that the primitive
matriarchate also existed in Spain, derived from the same
source as the Libyan matriarchate. She thus provides the
link between the theory of the Atlantic-island origin of the
Atlantean races and those who maintain that Atlantis never
existed except in North Africa.

She concludes her book by arguing from the artistic excellence of the prehistoric Iberian sculptures like the Lady of Elche in the Louvre and the elaborate dresses which the figures wore that the Iberian-Tartessian civilization was in some respects higher than that of Minoan Crete, which seems to have had certain features in common with it.

Spence's theory, supported by Mrs Wishaw's evidence of the high civilization of the Iberian-Tartessians, that Minoan Crete was a colony of Atlantis, or rather, the product of settlement by people with the tradition of Atlantis in their culture, is based on three considerations : that there is a strong resemblance between Minoan Crete and Atlantis as described by Plato; that Atlantis could not be an echo of Crete (see discussion of this problem on page 87) and that therefore Cretan civilization must contain elements of the more ancient Atlantean civilization; that there is a connection between Cretan and Aurignacian culture, which, together with the fact that the Cretans were largely of Iberian race, indicates that Cretan culture could have come from the west. The Atlantean elements in Cretan culture have already been noticed elsewhere. The connection with Aurignacian is not so obvious, but Spence thinks that the cultural descent is illustrated in the wall-paintings of Crete, its Tanagran statuettes, which link up with those of Spain by way of the Balearic islands, and particularly its cult of the bull which, as represented in Cretan palaces, is reminiscent of the art of the early

Aurignacian wall-painters. He thinks that the Cretan legend of the Labyrinth may be a sophistication of "some venerable myth of a tauric dwelling in a labyrinthine cave, and anciently derived from Spain or from the common source of Atlantis."

The Atlantean origin of Egyptian culture is inferred chiefly from a study of the ancient religious traditions of the Egyptians. The cult of Osiris, it should first of all be noticed, had certain rituals similar to rituals recorded in the Popul Vuh, a collection of the myths and history of the Quiche people of Central America from the time of their origin to the period of the Spanish conquest. The principal authority for modern knowledge of the Osiris cult is the ancient Egyptian *Book of the Dead*. The antiquity of this book is proved by the fact in 3,300 B.C. scribes who transcribed the ancient texts did not understand their purport. Professor Wallace Budge says that the earliest form of the work is contemporaneous with the founding of Egyptian civilization in the Nile valley; that is, says Spence, it was certainly not Egyptian. "All authorities are agreed that a large proportion of the stock which went to make up the composite people known as the ancient Egyptians had a western origin—that is, that their elements were the same as those which first entered Spain about 10,000 B.C. and which are known as Azilian-Tardenoisian." Egyptian civilization was therefore partly Atlantean and the Osirian religion was probably a Libyan importation. But can it be traced further west? It can, for the following reasons. (1) Aurignacian amulets buried with the dead are like those found on Egyptian mummies. (2) Shells were a symbol of life both in Egypt and in early Spain. (3) Reminiscences of Osirian worship are encountered all over west Europe and North Africa. "That it arrived at its apogee in Egypt is not denied. There it came into contact with other cults (Ra and Amen, from Asia), and borrowing, and amalgamation, unquestionably resulted therefrom, so that great complexity arose in the Osirian tradition. But in its simple and less complicated forms it is to be found in every country in western Europe. The Scottish and Old English ballads of John Barleycorn, for example, are nothing more or less than the myth of Osiris, the life and death of the barley plant in rural rhyme. Druidism is merely the cult of Osiris in another form, and the menhirs and dolmens of its architecture the rude parallels of the pyramid."

There is also an evident connection between the worship of Osiris and the legends and beliefs of ancient Britain. Druidism, which may have been brought by Iberian settlers from Spain has a number of Osirian features. The divine qualities attributed to mistletoe and to hazelnut milk show its connection with the milk-exuding fig of the sycamore associated with Hathor or Nut, the sky-goddess and mother of Osiris, sometimes worshipped as the divine cow. Another Osirian feature is the doctrine of the transmigration of souls, associated with Druidism; this is the probable reason why certain animals in ancient Britain were considered sacred. There are also a number of Osirian elements in the Arthur legend. King Arthur, who in his legendary form is probably a combination of a British general and a primitive culture hero, resembles Osiris in several respects. (1) In his story, like Osiris, he is murdered by a close relative and transported by wailing women in a boat to the island of the not-dead. (2) The island of Avallon, like the Osirian Aalu, is in the West; it is associated with Druids in old Celtic stories. (3) In the Grail story Arthur = Osiris = The Fisher King or fertility god. The myth of Horus (the son and possibly the resurrected form of Osiris) resembles that of Arthur and his Knights; both pledge themselves to wage war on evil monsters and both have the sun for a symbol, the sun in the Arthur story being typified by the Round Table. Most of Arthur's knights are old Celtic gods in disguise. For instance Merlin (says Professor Rhys) is the god of Stonehenge; and hence Arthurian legend is connected with Druidism.

From this Spence deduces that both Osirian and Druidical religion derive from Atlantean religion; both were spread by the Iberian descendants of the Azilians. Moreover, bull-worship and sacrifice (as described in Plato's Atlantis) are found both in the Egyptian cult of Apis (another form of Osiris, the calf of the divine cow Nut) and in the ancient Druidical rite of Beltane's fire in which bulls, sacred to the Druids, were sacrificed. On this evidence Spence asserts that the legends and traditions of the Celtic people consist of a substratum of Druid-Atlantean religion with a layer of later Celtic beliefs imposed upon them.

In the Celtic flood legends we have direct memories of the Atlantis cataclysm. The isles of the Blest in Irish legend (St. Brendan's Isle and Isle of Brazil) which are sometimes represented as being at the bottom of the sea and in mediaeval times confused with the Arthurian Avallon; the Irish and Welsh folk tales of cities under the water (Lough Neagh and Cardigan Bay) and the Breton legend of the submerged city of Ys, which is common to all branches of the Celtic people; the legend of Lyonesse, which is connected both with the legend of Ys and the Welsh account of the deluge caused by the bursting of Lake Llion ; and the tales of the pre-Celtic inhabitants of Ireland, the Firbolgs or Femorians (sometimes spoken of as men-from-under-the-water); all these connect up with the distribution of Atlantean-Druidical-Osirian religion and confirm in Spence's opinion the widespread diffusion not only of memories of the Atlantis cataclysm but also of the actual Atlantean culture.

(14)

Now this question of the three waves or culture-invasions which came from Atlantis to the shores of the old world must be considered in conjunction with that part of Spence's theory which deals with Atlantis in America, or rather, the American expression of what he calls the Atlantis culture-complex.

If a great continent stretching from Europe to America breaks up and disappears into the ocean we naturally expect waves of culture to be thrown upon both sides of that ocean. Assuming that the nature and diffusion of Atlantean culture in America can only be assessed by employing the European manifestation of it comparatively, do we find a similar invasion of the New World to correspond with the three waves of settlers in the Old, in such a place and at such a period as we can reasonably connect with the late submergence of the Antillian portion of the great Atlantic continent?

It may well be, says Spence, that the sub-continent of Antillia was not destroyed until 2,100 years ago. Be that as it may, we find about 200 B.C. abundant traces of the invasion of American soil by a high civilization which shows signs of having been developed from a culture similar to the Aurignacian. The origin of the people who carried it, the Mayas, is as mysterious as that of the Cro-Magnons. From archaeological research in Guatemala, Chiapas and Yucatan, it is evident that their art, even its earliest stages, was decadent, showing traces of disintegration and senility which indicate a very long period of existence. But the roots of Mayan civilization have not been found; and though authorities recognize that there have been new phases of their art since they entered Central America there is a complete absence of any primary evolutionary forms. Therefore it is necessary to look elsewhere for their place of origin.

A number of circumstances point to Antillia as the cradle of their culture. (1) Many authorities say they came from the West Indies or Antilles. (2) A wealth of tradition regarding a westerly and trans-oceanic connection existed in ancient Mexico and Central America all centred round the great mythical figure of the culture hero Quexacoatl (the feathered snake) and his people the Toltecs, who according to tradition were the peaceful invaders that brought the seeds of civilization to Mexico. Quexacoatl was worshipped by the Mayas as a god and leader of the Toltec race, but there is little doubt that Toltecs and Mayas were originally the same people and that Quexacoatl was really the leader of the first Mayan colonists to land in Mexico. For a long time it was thought that all the stories about the Toltecs and their great city Tollan which were current at the time of the Spanish conquest were entirely fabulous. But nowadays they are generally considered to be at least partly true. Particularly important is the fact that the history of Tollan, the city which the Toltec emigrants founded on Mexican soil, bears a close resemblance to that of Atlantis. According to a native chronicler it was founded in A.D. 536 on the site now occupied by the modern town Tula, north-west of the mountains which bound the Mexican Valley. The valley in which it stood was extremely fertile and known as the vale of fruits. The city, with its magnificent palaces and temples, took six years to erect. The Toltecs were skilled craftsmen and architects; the city walls were encrusted with rare red and black stones, the masonry was chiselled and laid out so that it resembled mosaic. The founder, Quexacoatl, was succeeded by a line

164

of able kings until in 994 the throne fell to Huemac II. At first this king ruled wisely, but later he became so degenerate that he lost his popularity and was threatened with revolt. The downfall of the city was foretold in many signs and portents. Like the Atlanteans the inhabitants began to incur the wrath of the gods by their love of pleasure and licentiousness, and a similar fate befell them. That winter all the crops and plants were killed by a severe frost and then followed a drought so severe that all the streams dried up and the *very rocks melted*. Plagues completed the disaster and the Toltecs were finally driven from the land by warlike tribes from the northern steppes. Mexico knew no more of them and their name and city lingered only as legend.

Such a disaster as this, says Spence, could not have happened on American soil, first because frosts so severe as those described in the legend could not possibly have occurred in those latitudes, and secondly because rocks do not melt even in the hottest suns; but they *do* melt under volcanic pressure, and he believes that the story of this catastrophe is really two stories confused, either by the Mexican chronicler or by the Toltecs themselves. It is a mixture of (1) a "venerable myth of catastrophe" of a volcanic nature current in Tollan, concerning the older city of Tlapallan whence the Toltecs originally came; and (2) the political break-up of the Toltecs under pressure of more virile northern tribes.

As to the personal myths of Quexacoatl, we may see in

them a "persistent memory of the arrival of a civilized race from the east, led by a chieftain of striking personality." In his godlike capacity Quexacoatl was connected with earthquakes and tempests. His father Citinatonali was regarded as the creator of heaven and earth, and in Mayan myth he is called "the old serpent who is covered with green feathers and who lies in the ocean." That is, Spence comments, he is the Mayan form of a sea god like Poseidon, the founder of Atlantis. Now Poseidon's son was Atlas, in Greek myth, Supporter of the Heavens. Citinatonali's son Quexacoatl is also represented as a sky supporter, both in Mexican manuscripts and in architecture, where he appears in caryatid form. Like Atlas, too, Quexacoatl was a twin. His connection with the sea is implicit in his name which means "Heart of the sea" and from the name of his wife Chalchihuitlicue, who was also a sea goddess. That the Mayas collectively were also connected with the sea is indicated by the study of Maya hieroglyphs which include among their symbols a conch shell and several others clearly related to a deluge.

We come now to the crux of Spence's whole theory, the Atlantis culture-complex. In his *History of Atlantis* (1928) he states categorically: "From the shores of western Europe to those of Eastern America a certain culture complex is distributed and is found on the intervening insular localities, while its manifestations are also to be discerned in great measure in North Africa and Egypt on the one hand, and in Mexico, Central America and Peru on the other. This complex is so constant in the region alluded to that it is clear now that a lost oceanic link formerly united its American and European extremities." It was introduced into the old world by the Cro-Magnons, Magdalenians and Azilians, and into the old world by the Mayas.

"The principal elements which distinguish the Atlantean culture-complex are the practice of mummification, the practice of witchcraft, the presence of the pyramid, head-flattening, the couvade,[10] the use of three-pointed stones, the existence of certain definite traditions of cataclysm, and several other minor cultural and traditional elements. The main argument is that these are all collectively to be found confined within an area stretching from the west coast of Europe to the east coast of America, and embracing the west Atlantic islands and the Antilles. So far as I am aware these elements are not to be found associated with one another in any other part of the world. This seems to imply the surest kind of proof that they must have emanated from some Atlantic area now submerged, which formerly acted as a link between east and west, and whence these customs were distributed east and west respectively."

The Aurignacians who painted the bones of the dead practised a rudimentary form of mummification and the kindred races of the Canaries practised a more advanced form of it resembling in some important details the Egyptian custom. Las Casas, Peter Martyr, and Columbus tell of mummification on the Antilles; in Haiti, Porto Rico and Santo Domingo. One myth of the Haiti Indians tells how a certain idol Faragavaol, was, like the mummified Osiris, discovered in the trunk of a tree. In Mexico, Peru and Central America there is often a close parallel with Egyptian funerary practice. The Mayas, for instance, buried the bodies of their kings and priests in elaborate stone sarcophagi accompanying them with canopic vessels. Like the Egyptians too, the Mayas associated certain colours with the principal bodily organs and with the cardinal points. Dogs were regarded as guides to precede the dead into the other world, just as Conubis did in the case of the dead Egyptian. A certain symbol associated with Egyptian mummies has also been found in Mayan MSS.

Similarly witchcraft, both in America and Europe seems to have been connected with the dead. Some of the Cro-Magnon rock-paintings strongly suggest that they had a cult of female sorceresses and some such cult is reflected among the Guanches of the Canaries. But in Mexico the cult is found in its entirety, Mexican witches behaving much as their European counterparts do. Tlazolteotl, for instance, is depicted wearing a peaked hat and riding through the air on a broomstick; elsewhere she stands beside a hut overhung with medicinal herbs and accompanied by an owl. Mexican witches, like European ones, also smear themselves with ointment to increase their speed through the air, and they indulge freely in orgiastic dances. They were actually called "witches" by the old Spanish friars who first wrote about them.

But the most important, indeed the central unifying part

168

of the culture-complex is the three-pointed thunderstone; it is the "hub of a wheel" of which witchcraft, mummification, and the idea of a magic tool in the hands of a divine shaper are the spokes. In Mexico, the planet Venus, the star of Quexacoatl, was regarded as a thunderstone and in many American and west European cities the symbol was wrapped in swathes of cloth precisely as if it were a mummy. Probably, when swathed, the powers of Thunder and the Tempest were symbolically dead, for in the western Irish island of Fladdahuan, if you unwrapped the bandages you "let loose a tempest." The thunderstone was also associated with the divine tool or pick, with which the gods fashioned the mountains and valleys, the shaping instrument of the primaeval mason. In Porto-Rico and Santo Domingo some curious three-cornered stones have been found carved in the shape of a mountain beneath which the head and legs of a recumbent buried figure protrude. These stones are evidently connected with the volcanic history of the islands and Spence supports the view that they were idols by citing the analogy of the Mayan conception of the universe, in which the earth is often supported by Quexacoatl, who so resembles Atlas and who is also Gucumatz the sea-dragon. In short he concludes that the stones represent a deity whose duty it was to uphold the universe, but who occasionally cast down his burden, thereby causing universal destruction and cataclysm.

(15)

Such is the only tolerable case for Atlantis, the Atlantic isle. Unfortunately it is not as strong as it may seem from the ethnological evidence.

Inevitably the chief pillar of the theory is the geological case for the existence of a Tertiary or Quaternary Continent late enough to be inhabited by *homo sapiens*. In the chapter on the geological evidence from which he draws his conclusions, Spence tends to make the case seem stronger than it really is. Though the names of a number of distinguished men of science are mentioned it is important to realize that the overwhelming majority of geologists do not believe in a continent existing late enough to have any connection with Plato's island. Scharff, Termier, Germain, Gregory and Hull are exceptions to the general rule. And when their various statements are examined in relation to one another there is no concensus of opinion as to the date or geographical position of such a continent. The nearest approach to a concensus is the extreme reserve which they all show directly they begin to talk in terms of an Atlantean rather than an Atlantic continent, and such conclusions as they have reached are stated with extreme caution. Termier appears to be the exception. "Geologically speaking," he says, "the Platonian history of the Atlantic is highly probable . . . it is entirely reasonable to believe that long after the opening of the straits of Gibraltar certain of these submerged lands still existed, and among them a marvellous island, separated from the

African continent by a chain of smaller islands. One thing alone remains to be proved—that the cataclysm which caused this island to disappear was subsequent to the appearance of man in Western Europe. The cataclysm is undoubted. Did men then live who could withstand the reaction and transmit the memory of it? *That is the whole question.* I do not believe it at all insoluble, though it seems to me that neither geology nor zoology will solve it. These two sciences appear to have told all they can tell, and it is from anthropology, from ethnography and lastly from oceanography, that I am awaiting the final answer." So even Termier shelves the final responsibility and we are left none the wiser.

It would also seem important as a basis for Spence's theory of a Maya-Atlantean culture-complex to show that an Antillian continent survived after the eastern or Atlantean continent disappeared; for unless we can assume this, we are again faced with the old difficulty of the disparity between the relative ages of the ancient civilizations of the old and new worlds. If both Maya and Egyptian civilizations are offshoots of Atlantean civilization, how do we account for the fact that the Egyptian version of it is at least 2,500 years older than the earliest Central American, except by supposing that the intermediate stages of Mayan culture were evolved on some western isle or islands which survived long after the disappearance of the Eastern Atlantic continent and are now sunk?

Unfortunately the geological case stated in Spence's

Atlantis in America is decidedly unsatisfactory and his whole theory is inevitably weakened as a result. Spence himself, however, does not admit that the Antillian part of his argument is essential. In a letter to the present writer, he states "I do not insist upon an Antillian continent and agree that the Mayas may possibly have been the descendants—far-off descendants—of refugees from Atlantis."

In addition to these doubts we must also weigh in the balance against Spence's hypothesis the theory of Continental Drift. According to this school of geologists the new and old worlds may be represented as the thick parts of the earth's crust resting in an unstable basic substance composed of silica and aluminium, and thus, like floating icebergs, slowly drifting apart. Alluding to it Spence writes: "The theory has been advanced that Atlantis may have been much closer to the European and American coasts at the date of its submergence than the present distance between these coasts would seem to imply, but it does not appear to me that the Atlantean hypothesis has anything to gain from such an admission." On the contrary the theory of Continental Drift tends, if anything, to destroy the Atlantean hypothesis since according to the computed rate at which the new and old worlds are at present drifting apart—300 miles in 10,000 years—Europe and America were joined only 80,000 years ago, *i.e.* in the Quaternary period.

Apart from the geological basis of Spence's theory, most

of the corroborative evidence is drawn from the analogy between the civilizations of Europe and America. From an elaborate comparison between them he deduces a littoral culture-invasion due to diffusion from a common centre in the Atlantic.

Against this attractive and well-argued thesis we have to weigh:

(1) The possibility of civilization having been carried round the other way, across the Behring Strait from the old world to the new. This is the explanation afforded by both principal schools of authoritative thought, the Diffusionists, who believe in one source for all cultures, and the supporters of Convergence. According to the Egyptian Diffusionists, who recognise the validity of the analogy between Egyptian and Mayan civilization, Egypt was the fountain of all civilization and its religious practices, arts and crafts were spread westwards to Africa, Spain and Britain and eastwards across central Asia and the Pacific to America by migrating tribes in search of gold and other metals. Spence has obviously been influenced by the work of Professor Elliot-Smith and Dr Perry (the chief Egyptian Diffusionists) though the conclusions he draws from similar evidence are totally different.

(2) The theory of Convergence, widely held nowadays, which supposes that similar cultures may be evolved quite independently; so that such apparently individual characteristics of civilization as pyramids, mummification, burial rites and cults of the dead, may be normal evolutionary

stages through which most primitive cultures pass, especially if they are evolved in similar environments.

Now as regards the origins of American culture, it is generally agreed that the *aboriginal* inhabitants of America came from somewhere else. On physical grounds an Asiatic origin is thought likely; and this is confirmed by geographical considerations, which show that primitive people who had not yet learned to use boats could easily have migrated to America across the frozen Bering Strait. But there is good evidence to show that the *higher states of American culture in the days before Columbus were developed independently on American soil;* and it is this consideration which must be taken into account in testing the validity of Spence's idea that the Mayas came from the Atlantic. Independent development is suggested by:— (*a*) The fact that early American culture seems to be based upon a plant indigenous to America, the maize plant. The evolution of its many cultivated varieties from the wild plant (which has not yet been discovered) suggests a long period of settled agricultural life in America which had no effect on the old world. This is reinforced by the domestication of the llama and alpaca in Peru and Bolivia. (*b*) The absence of old world cereals in America before the Conquest; of all domestic old world animals except the dog; of any knowledge of wheel traction, which was known in Mesopotamia in 4th millennium B.C. (note also the fact that Plato speaks of chariots in Atlantis); the ignorance of the potter's wheel, used in Elam and Mesopotamia also about 4000 B.C.

on that sunken continent in the west. But where the theory of Convergence really cuts into the Atlantean theory and Spence's arguments in particular is in its attack on the whole idea of a culture complex. Such cultural similarities as mummification and architecture between the civilizations of the old and new worlds can, say the opponents of a culture complex, be explained by the psychology common to all human beings, or by convergence dictated by natural and mechanical considerations. Mummification, for example can be suggested to primitive peoples by the natural preservations of bodies in a hot dry sandy soil such as the soil of Central America and Egypt.

Further doubts about the validity of Spence's Atlantean culture-complex theory are raised by his argument that the prehistoric and eastern elements in Celtic legends should be regarded as evidence of the Atlantean culture-complex in Britain. Here he makes the mistake of trying to clarify one mystery by another. Mysteries are centrifugal and Atlantis is the ideal centre for such unknown quantities as the Druids, the Arthur story and the Celtic Pantheon.

Actually, to reach Atlantis through the Celtic twilight is about as simple as getting to one of those remote islands of Arthurian legend which are accessible by two bridges, one running under water and the other a sword-edge! There is little doubt about the Egyptian and Aegean influences in Pre-Celtic Britain[11] and Ireland,[12] and there are obviously eastern elements in the Arthur romances,[13] which Spence calls "Atlantean" on the ground that they should be regarded not as "influences" but as evidence of a common cultural origin, as western and eastern branches of the same Atlantean tree. The objection to this becomes clear when we try to connect the two kinds of "influence," the early one revealed by Bronze Age archaeology, and other influences appearing in Celtic folklore and legend at a very much later date; also when we try to show that the Arthur story contains a historical tradition that can be directly related to remote archaeological periods in the west without reference to eastern influences in historical times. This is, of course, impossible. According to the evidence of some beads found at Stonehenge,[14] "Egyptian influence" was felt in Britain in the Bronze Age as early as 2,500 years ago, but it cannot be proved that the eastern characteristics which students of anthropology and folklore detect in our early literature were not incorporated at a much later date. For instance, the sources of the Arthur legend containing the Osirian-Atlantean elements referred to by Spence date only from the 12th century A.D., some 4,500 years later than the earliest indications of Osiris worship in the Delta and about 2,500 years later than the Stonehenge beads. There was plenty of time for those forms of the Osiris cult which appear to be reflected in the folk-literature of Britain to have been derived from Egypt by normal intercourse along trade routes or to have been brought from the east by migrating races, and it is therefore unnecessary to assume that eastern and western forms were derived from a common origin rather than from each other: and even if Osiris worship were known in Britain as far back as the Bronze Age it could still have been derived from the east by a process of "culture creep."[15] But there is no good evidence that any form of Osiris worship *was* known in Britain before the Celtic invasion and there is, on the contrary, plenty of reason to believe that most of the eastern elements in the Arthur story are much later. The late Jessie L. Weston, who showed that the Grail story could have been derived from the fertility cult of Tammuz (and thence, some think, from Osiris) said that it was brought to Britain in its higher form of Mithraism by Roman legionaries, but that after Christianity was introduced it was driven underground and secretly practised in caves and remote islands, surviving exoterically in folk traditions, mummers' plays, and sword dances. More recently Professor Lewis[16] has maintained that the Arthur story (in the Crétien de Troyes versions) represents distorted versions of Cretan and Mycenaean legends preserved by the Latin mythographers and brought from Rome or the east by returning bards or pilgrims in Christian times.

In any case Spence's assertion that Arthur *was* Osiris requires qualified acceptance. Opinion seems to be very divided on the question of the Osirian elements in the Arthur legends and it is by no means certain what exactly they are. The Celtic protagonists never tire of maintaining the western origin of those elements which seem to others to be suspiciously eastern, and the Egyptian Diffusionists, who have to find a billet for Osiris somewhere in Britain, tend to equate him with Merlin rather than Arthur. But it seems equally probable that Arthur, in his divine as opposed to his heroic capacity, is clothed in the frayed mantle of a native British culture hero, invented by Iberians, Celts or Celt-Iberians at heaven-knows-what date. The theory of Convergence again suggests that similar ideas might occur to primitive agricultural civilizations independently without their being gifted with any extraordinary originality. An indecisive battle of books has raged round this question for years, waged quite as hotly and with bigger guns of erudition than those which tend to misfire so noisily in the Atlantis controversy.

(17)

In adumbrating Spence's hypothesis little space has been devoted to the numerous Celtic legends of islands in the west and of cities under the water which he cites as folk memories of Atlantis. Suggestive as the tales are, they can hardly be of much value as evidence for the existence of Atlantis, the Lost Continent.

In the grey Celtic dawn streaking across the black night which succeeded the classical period, men thought they could just discern the dim outline of Atlantis far out to the west of the British Isles. They had many legends about it, but so full of wistful melancholy that it is difficult to connect them with Plato's island or any of the islands conceived by the geologists. Yet so persistently did they believe these legends that it is tempting to conclude

179

that memories of small local land subsidences really haunted the west, now in the guise of islands like St. Brendan's, Brazil and the Green-Island-under-the-Waves, now as Lyonesse and Avallon, now as the submerged cities seen by Bretons, Welsh and Irish, who could also hear the sound of church bells ringing. Many of these stories were doubtless due to the climate of the west. The shadowy outlines of the hills and headlands seen through mist and storm perhaps gave men cause to exercise their imagination as a substitute for the sun. Most people at one time or another have been deceived by low clouds and banks of mist into conjuring land out of vapours. Flying above the clouds in an aeroplane, how substantial they seem, as though one had only to land on them to remain in the clouds for ever. It is easy, too, to understand how sensitive innocent people inhabiting a land of hills and inland lochs would on calm days see towerlike hills reflected in the water and report that they had seen submerged cities. In Scotland the Gaels naturally looked to a Green Isle in the west, for Bride, the Spring goddess, to come and oust the hoary hag Bena who was responsible for the storms that raged upon their coasts during the winter months. Such are weather myths, as insubstantial as the mists and sunlight from which they were created.

But it is not so easy to account for a legend like that of St Brendan's Isle, which was so popular that it was translated into French, English, Welsh and Spanish, and so real to the Irish that six expeditions actually sailed west to look for it and arrangements were made for distributing the land when it should be discovered. There are state documents to prove this. And there was surely a burning faith behind the stout efforts of the saints to locate the Land of Promise. Cormac and Brendon both tried many times, and Brendon, according to the legend, succeeded only after he had been sailing for seven years. He found there feathered men, who in some versions are covered with hair. These were probably the original woodwoses, the mysterious wild men who at the end of the Middle Ages became so popular in European iconography that they are found as far south as the west door of the cathedral of Avila, rubbing shoulders with the very best saints and apostles.

In one story from the Scandinavian *Speculum Regale* Ireland itself is actually identified with Atlantis and is thought of as a land-under-the-waves. But the islands of the Irish saints do not seem to have much more in common with Atlantis than their position in the west. This is what Columcille said to the young men with a golden shoe on his foot who came seeking to compare his knowledge with the saint's:

"What is there beneath these islands to the west of us?"

And the young man replied: "There are underneath them tuneful long-haired men; there are well-shaped people both men and women; there are herds of deer, there are good horses; there are the two-headed, there are the three-headed, in Europe, in Asia, in an unknown green country from its border to its river mouth."

"That is enough so far," said Columcille.

The islands to which Maeldune voyaged belong even more to the geography of fairyland; there is the horse island, the island of birds, the island of ants, the island with the demon riders who held a horse race, the island of the fiery apple-eating pigs, the island with the wall of brass, the island with the wall of gold where lived the old man clad in the white hair of his own body. But none of the islands in this remarkable archipelago of Maeldune's Odyssey contain more than a single resemblance to Atlantis. And even if we must believe in a geological origin for these stories there is still no reason to refer them to the late Tertiary or early Quaternary continent. Nor can we legitimately deduce any evidence for the Atlantean case from the Celtic flood legends. Legends of cataclysm are common in the traditions of every race and it is surely idle to assign any group of them, let alone those of Western Europe, to a single source. Geology shows that many parts of the world now beneath the sea were dry land at some more or less remote date, and the deluge legends are therefore likely to have as many different sources as there were land submergences. Also it seems reasonable to suppose that a flood tradition caused originally by some local cataclysm would tend, by a process of oral diffusion or racial interpenetration to assume characteristics of other legends, thus gradually forming a group. Such traditions may of course carry with them memories of previous deluges, but it is obviously safer to refer them to the most recent local catastrophe. Let us take, for example, the group which contains, according to Spence, the legends of Lyonesse, Ys, and Lake Llion.

In Breton legend Ys was a fine city, situated in early Christian times on the shores of what is now the desolate Bay of Trespasses. Its ruler, the good and wise King Gradlon built a great wall between the city and the sea to save the city from being flooded by the high tides which threatened to swamp it. He alone kept the key of this sluice which was also the key of the city gate. In his piety Gradlon had only one sorrow: his beautiful daughter Dahut was extremely wicked. One night she stole the silver key while he slept and after committing many acts of folly attempted to escape from the city with her lover; but retribution overtook her. By mistake she opened the sluices and the sea poured in upon the city. Gradlon escaped only through the warning of St. Gwenole, which enabled him to leap on a horse and gallop away from the oncoming sea.

The legend of Lyonesse is somewhat similar. It was an island situated between Cornwall and the Scilly Isles. Tradition tells us that where the Atlantic now rolls there was once a large city the site of which is marked to-day by the group of rocks which are known as the "seven stones." There were many smaller towns and 140 churches. It was destroyed in a cataclysm. When the sea began to rise, one Trevilion managed to escape by mounting a swift horse and fleeing to the mainland. He was the sole survivor.

It is inevitable that the two stories should be connected. Lyonesse and Ys are geographically close to one another, and the legends are similar. Obviously too they must have some basis of fact. But why connect them with the sinking of the Quaternary Atlantic continent, when it is so much easier to account for them as a memory of the opening up of the English channel? Here is the obvious application of Dr Gidon's theory of the land submergences between Ireland and Brittany in the Bronze Age. Lyonesse can at any rate be partly accounted for by supposing that what is now the archipelago of the Scillies was once joined up to form a large island.

O. G. S. Crawford has described[17] how during the low spring tides in 1926 he found a long straight line of stones stretching across the uncovered sand-flats between Tresco and the uninhabited island of Samson. Closer investigation showed that the stones were the remains of a wall of human construction; some flint flakes were also found on the sand flats below the ordinary low water mark. The wall turned out to be a field hedge similar to others in various parts of the Scillies.

It is thought that these submerged sandflats were once a fertile and thickly populated land which became covered with sand and afterwards disappeared as a result of the general movement which lowered the whole shore of Brittany and Cornwall. The wall was probably uncovered by a tide scour which washed the sand away and being sheltered by its position from the pounding of the Atlantic waves outside it was preserved from erosion. The age of the remains is uncertain; but there is no proof that the

Scillies and Cornwall were inhabited before the Bronze Age. The possibility that the Scillies were still connected up as a single island as late as the 3rd century A.D. is suggested by the fact that Solinus, writing about 240, refers to them in the singular as "insulam Siluram."

O. G. S. Crawford does not, however, think that the legend of Lyonesse represents a traditional inheritance of the sinking of the coastline in the Iron Age. It is due, he believes, to intelligent induction on the part of unlettered fisherfolk who are capable of more acute observation than most educated people. Seeing a submerged wall, of which they did not know the origin, they might well conclude that it was the remains of a sunken city. But pure deduction would not help them to realize the slowness of geological processes and where they perceived evidence of sunken lands they would immediately attribute it to a cataclysm. Lyonesse is probably a case of imaginative interpretation; at any rate it seems futile to refer to it to the tradition of Atlantis.

(18)

But the geologists[18] tell us of another much greater flood, perhaps the greatest within the memory of mankind; and it happened, significantly enough, about 15,000 years ago when the Atlantic burst through the straits of Gibraltar and flooded the Mediterranean basin. This great change in the level of the Atlantic was caused by the melting, at the

185

end of the last Ice Age, of the Atlantic ice-packs which during the Pleistocene had drawn the waters northwards to swell the enormous glacier tongues then licking down towards the equator from the polar icecap. The loss of water involved in this freezing process had probably lowered the ocean level by several feet.

By the time of the melting of the ice the Aurignacian civilization had driven out the cannibal Mousterians from the west and was already in its higher neolithic stage. The tribes lived round the shores of the Mediterranean basin, which then consisted of two great lakes separated by a Sicilian land-bridge. When the overwhelming weight of the Atlantic flood burst open the straits and poured through the great flood-gates of Ceuta and Gibraltar it must have been the end of many thousands of Aurignacian settlers and their crops in the "Mediterranean Eden"; and in the minds of the survivors, driven north and south and east, there must have remained a tradition of cataclysm so vast and so terrible that it may well have lived in the memory of their descendants all over the world. . . .

That is the explanation of the story of Atlantis according to most modern geologists who will admit that Plato's story has any traditional basis at all.[19] They resolutely refuse to connect it with the Atlantic continent which disappeared, they say, far too early to make any impression on the mind of man, if indeed any type of man worthy of the name then existed on the earth.

Through a Glass Darkly

(19)

But despite this view, despite the numerous other objections mentioned in connection with the work of Lewis Spence, the Atlantean hypothesis still remains. Atlantis is a possibility, nothing more. And we have only to appreciate the enormous vagueness of our knowledge about the origins of man and the distribution of land and sea in remote geological periods in order to see the futility of making up our minds at this stage in the evolution of knowledge.

The results of recent oceanographic expeditions have forced the geologists to revise their opinions about the dating of the Atlantic shelves somewhat drastically and the present tendency is to date them later and later, though still not quite late enough. The question of continental shelves has been debated ever since Spencer[20] and Hull[21] showed that the beds of present day rivers on the Atlantic seaboard were continued across the ocean floor, ending in some cases thousands of feet below sea level. Some of the submarine valleys mapped by Spencer and Hull have since proved to have been hypothetical. On the other hand improved sounding apparatus has aided the discovery of a number of new ones. In fact, so many of these submarine canyons have been found that it looks as if they are a common characteristic of the outer margins of nearly all the continental shelves. There are many explanations of their origin; rift and fault action, submarine currents and stream erosion. F. P. Shepherd,[22] who accompanied the U.S.A. coastal survey ship that recently charted the Georges Bank west of Cape Cod and the Gulf of Maine supports the last of these theories, that the canyons were formed at a time when the surrounding land was above sea level. "A new suggestion that I wish to propose is that the valleys were originally cut by rivers but submerged a long time ago and filled in with sediment during the cutting and building of the present continental shelves, being subsequently reopened from time to time by great landslides." This seems to indicate a date too remote to have any significance for the Atlantean hypothesis. But more recent results obtained by the Woods Hole Institute Research ship *Atlantis* make one wonder. Dredges towed along the slopes of the Georges Bank Canyons brought up fossiliferous rocks of the late Tertiary period, which suggests that the rock strata may have been cut out by stream erosion (*i.e.* by a river) *since* the late Tertiary period. Commenting on this possibility, H. C. Stetson[23] points out that the sinking of the canyons to their present level would mean either a terrific uplift movement of the coastline or a "world wide lowering and rising of the sea level of enormous extent . . . this relative shift, amounting to more than 8,000 feet, must have occurred since the late Tertiary," in other words, in the pleistocene period of the Quaternary. But Stetson hesitates to accept this explanation because it is contrary to generally accepted theories and because "*a fall and rise of sea level of the order of magnitude which the evidence demands, coupled with the shortness of time within which it must have taken place, approaches the catastrophic . . .*"

Through a Glass Darkly

On this dramatic note the question of the geological case for Atlantis must be put back on its continental shelf for the problem of the submarine versus the subaerial origin of the canyons is still at the time of writing, regarded as open and there is no use in reaching conclusions which are not yet considered by experts to be justified by the evidence. But if it can in the future be shown that tracts of the Atlantic were dry land in the Quaternary period (500,000 years ago) then will be the time to reconsider the whole question—in the light of the latest knowledge about the age of man. Recently scientific opinion on this question has been completely revolutionized by the results of Dr Leakey's researches in Kenya, where he has discovered skulls dating from the middle Pleistocene[24] (250,000 years ago); and these skulls show that even at that almost incredibly remote period, in Africa at any rate, there was a type of true *homo sapiens* in existence. So that though the ends do not yet meet, it is by no means impossible that they soon will if the present tendency, for the dating of the Atlantic bed to become later as man gets older, continues. Geologists once thought that the Atlantic had remained in its bed since the beginning of time, just as man was believed to have been created in 4007 B.C.

"The eye of a geologist," says M. Termier, in a very ungeological digression, "is sensitive to very vague and very uncertain lights which illuminate, for him alone, the night of the Deep and the blacker night of the remote past . . ."

189

And so we are back where we started. The harder one tries to discover the solution of the Atlantis problem the clearer it becomes that no solution is possible until the sciences upon which it depends become a great deal more developed. It is impossible honestly to be entirely satisfied either way about the existence of an Atlantic island from which Plato might have derived the nucleus of his fable. Taking the strictly minimalist point of view it may be concluded that while a study of Plato and his sources gives us cause to *look* for a real or traditional Atlantis, the *available* evidence from geology, archaeology or ethnography does not yet justify the belief that such an island is there to be found, and the majority of scientists declare that it never will be. The former conclusion owes perhaps something to the essentially human tendency to rationalize what one wants to believe, just as the scientific refusal to accept the possibility of Atlantis is somewhat conditioned by the stout efforts of scientists to dehumanize themselves and steel their understanding against the appeal of romance. And so the clash takes place and the sparks fly. "Moonstruck dreamers," say the scientists. "Blind materialists!" the Atlantophils reply. But both are ultimately wasting their time in trying to refute each other, for the process involves an intuition-perception antithesis which is about as futile as the opposition between science and religion. One side says: "I feel the truth of Atlantis and therefore I believe in it," and the other replies: "I don't perceive it, therefore it is not there to be perceived."

Through a Glass Darkly

Some scientists fail to perceive the basic difficulty and continue to delight in exposing the manifest sophistries and lapses of logic in their opponents' arguments. Another group which is sufficiently clear-sighted to have observed that the majority of Atlantean protagonists base their case on "faith," recognise that further dispute is idle and prefer to preserve a dignified and superior silence. In the view of this latter group the frequent and thinly disguised attempts to present conclusions reached intuitively in terms of rational argument from exact knowledge are sufficient to discredit the whole Atlantean hypothesis.

But here, it seems, an important issue is at stake. What is the value of intuition, if any? Later on we shall see that the occultist writers on Atlantis use this approach as a legitimate basis for historical "knowledge." We cannot entirely discredit the method until we know more about the human mind and the possibilities of folk-memory, for it is not impossible that certain folk memories may be transmitted subconsciously and esoterically, appearing now and then on the surface in the form of strong irrational intuitions about the truth of certain events in the remote past. Some such theory would explain certain aspects of "faith." What was once a living oral tradition may still persist, transmuted by time into a belief in the historical truth of a written legend.

THEN FACE TO FACE

(1)

The theosophists, anthroposophists, yogis and other kinds of occultists form a Popular Front on the question of Atlantis. In contrast to the main body of Atlantophils they are extraordinarily unanimous in their conception of it. They care nothing for scientific discussions; Atlantis is an integral part of their system of evolution and a fact beyond dispute. They know all about it, when, where, how. But they tell a very different story from Plato.

The ground is prepared by a general attack of the occultist Popular Front against the orthodox methods of arriving at knowledge of prehistory. All evidence derived through our sense, they say, is untrustworthy. This is shown by the fact that history is never constant; the prehistory of one age becomes the history of the next. But those who rely on the methods of initiation are able to find the historical Absolute. The internal is the eternal, the external or material is merely a falsehood in the process of becoming a truth, in obedience to the constant adjustments required by the progress of sciences like archaeology, ethnology and geology.

The eternal, of course, is not accessible by sense perception but it is accessible by the "Akashic Records," a mysterious store of historical knowledge, the accuracy of which is acknowledged by all the occult schools. Rudolf

Steiner asserts that the story of Atlantis forms several chapters of the Akashic records. Occultists also claim that a direct tradition of Atlantis still survives as the cherished secret of a little band of initiates. There are, writes Madame Blavatsky, "a handful of thoughtful and solitary students who pass their lives in obscurity far from the rumours of the world, studying the great problems of the spiritual and physical universes. They have their secret records in which are preserved the fruits of the long line of recluses whose successors they are . . . these men believe the story of Atlantis to be no fable, but maintain that at different epochs of the past, huge islands, and even continents, existed where now there is but a wild waste of waters. In these submerged temples and libraries the archaeologist would find, could he but explore them, the materials for filling in all the gaps that now exist in what we imagine is *history*." L. P. Sinnett in his preface to Scott-Elliott's *Story of Atlantis* describes the work as "a pioneer essay of the new method of historical research," which is "astral clairvoyance"; much of the information in the book is derived from secret "records" and "maps" which are open to be inspected by the "duly qualified."

(2)

Before Atlantis was Lemuria,[1] a continent that occupied a large part of what is now the South Pacific Ocean. Atlantis, according to Scott-Elliot's first map, which shows it 1,000,000 years ago, extended "from a point a few degrees

193

east of Iceland to about the site now occupied by Rio de Janeiro in South America. Embracing Texas and the Gulf of Mexico, the Southern and Eastern states of America, up to and including Labrador, it stretched across the ocean to our own islands—Scotland and Ireland and a small portion of the north of England forming one of its promontories—while its equatorial lands embraced Brazil and the whole stretch of ocean to the African Gold Coast." Then, part of Lemuria and the fragments of the even older Hyperborean continent were still existing. At this time, the Miocene, the first of the great Atlantean cataclysms occurred 800,000 years ago. This submerged the northern part of Atlantis, separating the now growing American continent from its parent Atlantean continent, making Atlantis an independent continent occupying the bulk of the Atlantic ocean from about 50 degrees North to a few degrees South of the Equator. Meanwhile Lemuria was also decreasing in size.

The next catastrophe took place about 200,000 years ago and was "relatively unimportant." As a result of it the straits of Gibraltar were opened up and the Atlantic which had hitherto covered West Africa was extended right across the Sahara to Egypt. Atlantis itself was now split into two halves, called Ruta and Daitya.

The most stupendous of all the cataclysms happened about 80,000 years ago. As a result the world became much as we know it. The differences were that the Atlantic still stretched across the Sahara to the borders of Egypt with a northern outlet into the Mediterranean between Alexandria and east Tripolitana, and the Baltic was still non-existent. Daitya, the smaller and more southerly of the two Atlantean islands had almost disappeared, while Ruta had decreased to the relatively small island of Poseidonis. As Poseidonis, Atlantis remained apart from minor changes from 75,000 years ago until 9564 B.C. at which date the final catastrophe happened, and the world became "normal."

The original Atlantean stock came from Lemuria and was evolved from the survivors of the general racial decadence which affected the Lemurians in the last stages of their evolution. The decadent race-types of Lemuria still persist to-day as savages in many parts of the world.

In time the mass of the Atlantean race also became decadent, and from a select division of them sprang the Aryan race. Lemurians, Atlanteans and Aryans are root-races of humanity. Before the Lemurians arrived the world had already known two root-races, and two more root-races will succeed the Aryan in the future. By the time that the picture of man's evolution has been completed there will have been seven root-races in all; one always succeeds another as in the Lemurian, Atlantean, Aryan sequence, and each root-race has physical and mental characteristics totally different from those of the preceding one.

Each root-race itself passes through seven stages of evolution; but one stage does not necessarily disappear as soon as the next begins to arrive, and these sub-races are apt to overlap. "Thus there are always dwellers on the earth, living side by side, but showing the most varied stages of evolution."

The first sub-race of the Atlanteans arose from the last remnant of the Lemurians who were capable of further evolution. In general the Lemurians were very different from the Atlanteans. They could make mental images of things, but they could not preserve them as memories. Only in the final stages did they begin to evolve speech. Nevertheless they had a certain civilization. They had houses and tools, and their minds worked with instinctive efficiency.

The Atlanteans in turn were very different from the Aryans, in their physical appearance, in mental capacity and in their civilization. They could not reason or calculate, but in place of these faculties they had a highly developed memory. The Atlantean did not calculate by mathematical symbols but by remembering a former precedent; his mind was a storehouse of pictures for reference and for comparison. All education consisted in teaching children not to think but to remember, and when new sets of circumstances arose they just had to experiment. This produced a uniformity of life and gave very little scope for progress in the modern sense. In decisions of importance reliance was placed upon those who had lived long enough to have acquired great experience and who were gifted with retentive memories. From this reliance upon memory, however, they derived a certain important quality. They were masters of the "life-force." As we use coal or electricity for warmth and energy, so the Atlanteans were able to go right back to the germinal force of things for the energy required for their technical works. They could harness growing-power for heating, locomotion, etc. Life-force, for instance, propelled their airships; this was made possible by the rarefied atmosphere which surrounded the earth at that time, but it meant also that the airships could only fly a few hundred feet above the ground and much slower than the aircraft of to-day. Another feature of the physical world of the Atlanteans was that water was much more fluid than it is to-day and this lack of density enabled life-force in seeds to be used as motive power in their hydraulic works. The physique of the Atlantean was also different; he had absolute control of his physical forces and within him he had the means of increasing them at will by the action of life force upon the water in his body. (Evidently the Atlanteans were not, like we Aryans, slaves to irresponsible glands!)

Even the outward expressions of collective life were different from ours. Towns were not settlements in the modern sense but like organic growths. "A settlement resembled a garden in which the houses formed themselves out of trees of which the branches were intertwined in a realistic manner." This "natural" ordering of life was accompanied by a social sense which, recognizing the common root of all things, had no idea of private property, an invention due to the development of reasoning power.

The first Atlantean sub-race is known as the Rmoahal. According to Scott-Elliot they originated in Lemuria and emigrated to Atlantis. Rmoahals became a race 4,000,000 or 5,000,000 years ago, were of average stature of ten or twelve feet, and were mahogany black in colour. Rudolph Steiner, who concentrates on the "soul life" of our Atlantean fore-fathers, tells us that Rmoahals developed especially the powers of speech which had for them a strange natural force. Words were truly magical. "When a Rmoahal pro-nounced a word, this word developed a force akin to that of the object described by it. Hence it is that words had the power of healing at that time, and that they could hasten the growth of plants, tame the rage of animals and produce other such effects." Subsequent Atlantean sub-races had not this magical power. Rmoahals considered speech divine. They were naturally religious and regarded speech as the operation of nature working divinely in them.

Atlantean sub-race number two was a hardy reddy brown race which originated on an island off the west coast of Atlantis and migrated to the mountainous district of Atlantis corresponding with the part that afterwards became Poseidonis, driving the native Rmoahals north. They had a kind of kingship to unify their communal life and their spiritual life centred round their ancestors whom they worshipped. They were heroic conservatives who measured the success of the present only by past standards and got communal uplift from memories of fine deeds performed by their ancestors. The third sub-race is called Toltec. It emerges at the most glorious period of Atlantean history, hailing from the western part of

Atlantis which split off from the rest after the cataclysm of 800,000 years ago and became the American continent. "So dominant and so endowed with vitality was this race that inter-marriages with the following sub-races failed to modify the type, which still remained essentially Toltec; and hundreds of thousands of years later we find one of their remote family races ruling magnificently in Mexico and Peru, long ages before their degenerate descendants were conquered by the fiercer Aztec tribes from the north." Like the Tlavatlis they were red brown people but more coppery. They were tall and well built with somewhat Grecian features.

According to Mrs Besant (*The Pedigree of Man*, 1908) who generally goes one better than Scott-Elliot, the Toltecs were 27 feet high and their bodies were "of a hardness sufficient to bend a bar of iron were it launched against them, or to bend a bar of steel, were they heavily struck by it; one of our knives would not cut their flesh, any more than it would cut a piece of present-day rock."

The Toltec territory extended right across the continent and their capital was on the east coast of Atlantis.

They were the first race to organize their society into a commonwealth. Hereditary kingship began and "that which had formerly continued only in the memory of their fellow men, the father now transferred to the son." In actual fact the father was able to transfer his gifts to his son by educating him in such a way that he handed over his personal accumulation of life pictures and made him instinctively

199

rather than intellectually able. This business of collecting life pictures was really a philosophy of knowledge in the form of personal experience and the selection of a king was made by wise initiates on this basis. The king was himself an initiate and had power over the people which was almost god-like in its effect. Unfortunately the kings began to abuse this power and used it selfishly, thus destructively. Use of power for selfish ends became very developed in the next sub-race, the fourth or Turanian. This was the age of the irresponsible individual, who sacrificed the common good to his own uncontrolled impulses. They were, however, great colonisers and from the earliest days they had been migrating to the lands which lay to the east of Atlantis. They were native to the great central regions of Atlantis west and south of the Tlavatli region, but they shared a good deal of their territory with the Toltecs.

The fifth sub-race, the Semites, was a turbulent discontented lot always warring with their neighbours, especially the Akkadians, already a growing power by the time the second map period was reached. They came from the more southerly of the two north-eastern peninsulas, corresponding to what is now Scotland, Ireland and part of the surrounding sea. They developed logical thought as a check to the havoc wrought by selfish individualism. Thoughts by now had taken the place of pictorial images stored in the mind, and they formed a short cut to the logic involved in comparing and organising these memories. Thought power also enabled them to develop a conscience or "inner

voice" which saved a lot of tiresome remembering; but at
the same time man was losing his control over the forces
of nature, and the mastery of the life force waned.

Out of the most gifted section of this fifth sub-race was
formed the nucleus of the fifth root-race, the Aryans, whose
evolutionary destiny is to perfect the power of thought. This
transition from the fifth sub-race of the Atlantean root-race
to the first sub-race of the Aryan root-race was achieved
under the guidance of semi-divine prophets, spirits who had
assumed human form and acknowledged the leadership
of one of their number called the Manu. The Manu saw
in the Semite development of thought-power the best material among all the Atlantean races for the formation of a
new root-race, and selecting a few of the rarest thinkers,
segregated them in a suitable spot in Central Asia where
they were free from the contaminating influences of less
worthy stock. "Men were now meant to understand the
divine powers which they had formerly followed blindly.
So far, the Gods had led men through their messengers;
henceforth men should know of these divine Beings. They
were to consider themselves as executive organs of Divine
Providence. The Divine Leader lived among them in human
form and taught them to worship not human forms of
divine king-leaders as formerly, but the unseen powers, not
representable by any 'graven image'." They began, under
the tuition of the Manu, to appreciate the abstract and to
place less reliance on the anthropomorphic. When the Manu
was satisfied with his human initiates, he withdrew and left
them to carry on alone.

The same process characterises the transition from each root-race to its successor and will continue to operate until the full complement of seven races brings the human race to perfection.

The sixth or Akkadian sub-race originated after the catastrophe of 800,000 B.C. at about 40°N. 10° E. The Akkadians overran Atlantis and fought with the Semites, whom they vanquished about 100,000 years ago, then set up a dynasty in the old Semite capital. They were an enterprising colonial and commercial people with a constant desire for novelty and change; but they were also prudent and their leaders were chosen for wisdom rather than for deeds. They were the first legislators.

Prudence was further developed in the seventh and last Atlantean sub-race, the Mongols. But though they were thoughtful they remained true to the sense of memory in that the oldest were still considered the wisest. They had little power over the life-force, but the quality survived as a strong belief in the existence of such a power which was a kind of god to them. They were a mystical people. Their stock developed on the plains of Tartary from descendants of the Turanian colonists and differed from all other Atlantean sub-races in that they had connection with the mother continent.

All these Atlantean sub-races migrated and sub-divided, resulting in the racial complex of the present time. Perpetual migration from Atlantis was guaranteed by three causes; desire for colonies, over-population and the fear of cataclysms.

Then Face to Face

The highest Atlantean civilization was that developed by the Toltecs, who achieved a federal system ruled over by an adept emperor. The dynasty was divine, and recruited from a lodge of initiates. The golden age of the Toltec empire lasted 10,000 years; then things began to go wrong. Priests and kings began to use their power malevolently. Black magic and witchcraft spread through the land. The kings took part in phallic rites and set up images of themselves for public worship. They bred loathsome monsters, which were enslaved with the worst types of elemental. A "black" rebellion drove the initiate emperor from the City of the Golden Gates and a rival was set up in the city. The "white" emperor was forced to take refuge in the seat of one of his tributary Toltec kings. Meanwhile the power of his rival increased and millions were converted to the black arts, while many "white" sympathisers, realising that a catastrophe was at hand, emigrated to foreign lands.*

In due course a great cataclysm came. The wicked inhabitants of the City of the Golden Gates were swept to their death by the Atlantic waves and the "black" civilization was nearly annihilated. But the Black Arts survived, notwithstanding the terrible lesson of the past, through four successive cataclysms, until the coming of the final and inevitable catastrophe which destroyed Poseidonis and to a great extent purified the world. Throughout this period there was always a "white" emperor in Atlantis who upheld the good right up to the very end.

*See Appendix A. An Atlantean ghost.

Mention has already been made of the Toltec migrations led by priests who anticipated the approaching cataclysms. The most important was that which led to the founding of the First Dynasty in Egypt. After the Golden Age of the Toltec empire was over and the first great catastrophe had failed to exterminate the black arts, the "white" initiates decided that purer surroundings were required and so a whole lodge was transferred to Egypt. The country at that time was thinly populated and conditions were favourable for the planting of a new civilization.

210,000 years ago the Divine Dynasty of Egypt was founded. Colonists were brought from Atlantis and during the next 10,000 years the two great pyramids of Gizeh were built, as "permanent halls of initiation" and as shrines for some great talisman to be used in the forthcoming catastrophe prophesied by the initiates. In the catastrophe of 200,000 years ago Egypt was flooded, but after a long period it emerged and was again peopled by the descendants of its Atlantean inhabitants who had retired during the flood to the Abyssinian mountains, then an island in the Arabian sea. The race type was modified by fresh Akkadian colonists from Atlantis. The country was again temporarily inundated in the Atlantean cataclysm of 80,000 years ago and the only buildings which survived were the pyramids. Then began the third Divine Dynasty and the early kings built the temple of Karnak and many of the other ancient buildings which are still extant.

The ensuing period, leading up to the final cataclysm

which submerged Atlantis and caused another tidal wave
to sweep over Egypt, seems to have been chiefly remarkable
for the rise of the cult of Osiris. According to the occultist
Paul Brunton[2] we must reject the official legend of Osiris,
the "fantastic incredible myth" of the murder, the hacking
into pieces and the putting together again. After "dangling
the plummet of his mind into the problem . . . out of
the silence of the past came this reply":—Among the
Atlantean emigrés during the decadence was the god-king
Osiris seeking pastures new for his "younger spiritual kith
and kin" in Egypt. "The party under Osiris' immediate
direction was taken to prehistoric Egypt, on whose
shores they halted before presently sailing up the Nile,
passing the pyramids and the Sphinx, products of the
first Atlantean outflow, until Osiris bade them stop, not
far from the present site of Abydos." There they settled
and were peaceably accepted by the native population
who were glad to be taught by them. After Osiris died his
cult was handed down and long afterwards, when his
teaching required recodifying, another teacher, Thoth,
arose and established a second centre of Osirian mysteries
at Sais. But by the time the final tidal wave swept over
Egypt at the sinking of Poseidonis, the Lodge of Initiates
had already been transferred elsewhere and the Divine
Dynasty was at an end.[3]

(3)

On the details of life on Atlantis the occultists are very
informative. Some of these details seem to us surprisingly

modern; such are gas-bombs and high explosives, sex-equality and co-education. "Airboats," writes Scott-Elliot, "may be considered as the private carriages of these days, or rather the private yachts, if we regard the relative number of those who possessed them, for they must at all times have been difficult and costly to produce." At the end of the Golden Age battleships navigating the air replaced the seaships; they could carry 50 to 100 fighting men. Arts and sciences flourished, and alchemy was practised with such success that the quantity of precious metals was unlimited. Science was taught to the advanced intellects, but the chief object of education was to train the psychic faculties and to probe the hidden forces of nature. The occult properties of plants, metals and precious stones were taught, as well as transmutation. But the masses were not even taught to read and write; they had a purely technical training in handicrafts or agriculture. There were colleges of agricultural research which evolved new cereals by crossing those that existed with the grasses of the earth; in this manner they achieved the evolution of the plantain from a kind of elongated melon filled with seeds.

In the matter of food and drink the Atlanteans seem to have been less enlightened. They ate, among other things, decomposing fish; and they drank hot animal blood. The adept kings and the priesthood of Initiates however were purely vegetarian. A certain highly intoxicating liquor was also at that time in vogue, but the populace got so drunk that prohibition had to be introduced.

The City of the Golden Gates was much the same as the Atlantean citadel described by Plato. But Plato seems to have omitted to mention that there was a "strangers' home," a palace where all strangers who came to the city were entertained free at the expense of the government.

In the days before the decadence poverty was almost unknown in Atlantis, despite the high population. The prosperity was chiefly due to their system of land tenure. Land was nationalized in the sense that it belonged, with all the stock on it, to the adept Emperor. It was divided into districts administered by an official who was responsible to the emperor for the well-being of the district; produce was collected and redistributed to be consumed, for the most part, in the districts in which it was farmed; but a small amount was set apart from the upkeep of the Emperor and the City of the Golden Gates and occasional exchanges were arranged between districts in the event of necessity. On the whole, however, the districts were the "concern" of their inhabitants and any increase of productive capacity meant an extra "dividend" for the "shareholders." A high rate of productivity was assured by the psychic powers of the administration, who in collaboration with the astronomer-adepts, were able not only to tell the peasants the exact time to sow and reap but also if necessary to influence the weather.

It remains to describe religion in Atlantis. In Rmoahal days the people were ruled by a divine Manu and the state was perfect. When the Manu died he became a god and his memory was universally preserved. In Tlavatli days this developed into sun worship; the sun, giver of light, symbolized the supreme Being. Monoliths were built in great circles, a custom to which the Akkadians reverted in later days when they built Stonehenge. In Toltec times the sun-disk was the only image of the deity permitted, but subsequently there was a reversion to the purer Manu worship when people worshipped images of the archetypal man as the highest representation of the divine. The Turanian Age, the age of irresponsible individualism, abused this form of worship until it degenerated to the point when rich men worshipped gorgeous statues of themselves which were kept in elaborate shrines tended by private priests. Devils were invoked with the aid of brutal blood sacrifices and they too were worshipped. These were the evil days and in accordance with eternal laws they reaped their harvest of cataclysm.

(4)

In considering the occultist conception of Atlantis it would be irrelevant to show how it all fits in with their theory of eternal cycles, the descent of spirit into matter and the re-ascent of matter into spirit. It is enough to say that Atlantis is an integral part of their philosophic and religious system. And whatever we think of their methods of arriving at these conclusions or the conclusions themselves from an objective point of view, a study of them tells us a lot about Atlantis: which is all that is required.

Then Face to Face

To the non-initiate it looks as if most of the foregoing story could have been concocted without any recourse to psychic powers, by commonsense induction, flagrant disregard of historical data and a fertile imagination stimulated by fairly wide reading. The account of the institutions of the Atlanteans has all the appearances of the conventional Utopia. Such important characteristics of it as the divine monarch, the architecture of the City of the Golden Gates and the communistic system of land tenure could very easily have been derived from a casual acquaintance with Plato's *Timaeus* and *Critias* and the *Republic*, More's *Utopia*, and Augustine's *De Civitate Dei*, the whole brought up to date according to the principles of 19th century socialism. For some of the details of the Atlantean civilization we do not even have to credit the theosophists with imagination. "The most notable achievement," says Scott-Elliot, "to be recorded of the Atlantean agriculturists was the evolution of the plantain or banana. In the original wild state it was like an elongated melon with scarcely any pulp, but full of seeds as a melon is. It was of course only by centuries (if not thousands of years) of continuous selection and elimination that the present almost seedless banana was evolved." This observation comes straight from Donelly's *Antediluvian World* published only a few years before (1882), in which Donelly, working on the data of Professor Kunzte, concluded that the banana must have been cultivated on Atlantis and carried east and west by civilized Atlantean colonists. Again, the explanation of the

Osiris myth, though in complete accord with the general occultist theory of the Atlantean migrations, completely disregards the mass of evidence which points to a totally different origin. And the description of the tree-like architecture of the early Atlantean houses suggests a palpable debt to Grimm's *Fairy Tales* as illustrated by Arthur Rackham.

In short "probability" is the last word the non-initiate would think of applying to the occultist conception of Atlantis. And yet, it is a curious fact that the marvellous tale they tell does seem to have anticipated certain scientific theories. First, in regard to the extreme age of *homo sapiens* in their scheme of evolution. The recent scientific discoveries of Dr Leakey (see page 189) tend rather to justify this, and it looks as if further 'discoveries may completely alter our conception of "Adam's ancestors." Again, there is a strong resemblance between the occultist conception of Lemuria and Atlantis and the two Atlantean continents recognized by Karst, the Lemuria of the occultists corresponding to Karst's proto-Atlantis. In some respects, too, their geological scheme seems to be in striking agreement with that of Professor Suess, of Vienna. In his *The Face of the Earth* (trans. Sollas, Clarendon Press, 1906) he writes, in the section on palaeozoic seas: "From the following, however, it will appear that this continent (a vanished palaeozoic Atlantis) persisted as such up to a very recent epoch in the history of the earth . . "

"We have recognized the existence of two continents, of

which only fragments are visible at the present day. The first occupied the position of the north Atlantis ocean, as is indicated by the nature and distribution of the paleozoic sediments in Europe and America. Greenland is a remnant of it. This ancient continent is the *Atlantis*.

"The second continent, first clearly discernible towards the close of the carboniferous period, is now represented by three fragments, Africa, India and Australia. As Greenland on the one hand, so the Indian peninsula on the other projects into the ocean which covers the subsided table-lands. This continent is Gondwana land."[4] But the occultists call it Lemuria. Then there is the occultist conception, dating from the last century, of Atlantis slowly disintegrating in a series of four cataclysms and at one time split into two islands Ruta and Daitya. This anticipates Spence's theory of the three Atlantean cataclysms and the two Atlantean islands Atlantis and Antillia. Lastly, without being far-fetched, we may notice a tendency for the occultists to regard the City of the Golden Gates in the same way as Frobenius regards the Nigerian Benin, as the sum of a series of migrations, an ethnological picture in which the characteristics of many different Atlantean periods are summed up as a whole.

One part of the occultist story, which concerns the British origin of the Semites and Stonehenge, is evidently an echo of the quaint 18th century scientific theories which so influenced Blake and produced the Jerusalem myth. And perhaps, as we shall try to show later, the myth appeals to modern occultists for the same reasons, national pride and the conception of race as a unifying and binding principle.

But in the main the occultist Atlantis seems to be the best possible illustration of what, in the catch-phrase of the psychologists, is called wish-fulfilment. The strength of their belief in the Golden Age that has been and may return, the perfect state in which purity and spiritual grace are united, is no doubt partly due to a subconscious desire to restore the psychic equilibrium which has somehow been upset by their inability to adapt themselves to the conditions of modern life. This aspiration, as Alexander Bessmertny has pointed out, can be shown to be in different degrees the basis of every approach to Atlantis, whether intellectual or intuitive.

There are several reasons for the specially wish-fulfilment character of the occultist Atlantis. The lack of authoritative scientific backing for the Atlantean hypothesis naturally commends the study of it to the occultists, for they themselves steer a somewhat precarious course between science and orthodox religion, acknowledged by neither and despising both. Also the mysterious paradisaic quality of the Atlantis legend makes it peculiarly suitable for elucidation by extra-sensible means without fear of direct contradiction from science, which cannot pretend to be absolutely certain about it. Atlantis is the Mecca of all initiates. It is like the secret rose of the Yeatsian mysticism. "I will tell you of myself," says the Knight in the Secret Rose, "for now I am the last of that fellowship, I may tell all and witness for God. Look at the Rose of Rubies on my helmet, and see the symbol of my life and hope . . . at last came there a great Rose of Fire and a voice out of the Rose had told him how men would turn from the light of their own hearts, and bow down before outer order and outer fixity, and that then the light would cease, and none escape the curse except the foolish good man who could not, and the passionate wicked man who would not, think." The truth for Yeats as for Blake lies in the ancient way somewhere concealed in the essence of the corrupted world, and the truth may only be revealed by "sages standing in God's holy fire" for they are the "singing masters of the soul." The occultists are the true Atlantean romantics and no one with a grain of optimism in him can deny the attractiveness of the possibility, so constantly stated by occultists to be a fact, that an Atlantean flame still burns kept alive by some society of initiates who have inherited the guardianship of the arcane tradition from generations of forgotten sages. There is a tradition of Atlantean worship, perhaps, a mere fragment of something quintessential and precious, like a gram of radium concealed in a mountain of rubbish; a tradition more surely representative of the life which drove the people of Atlantis to work and play, to make love and to laugh, than any that could ever be deduced from the united results of the researches of all the archaeologists, ethnologists, mythologists and other -ists.

VAST SHADY HILLS

(1)

Blake and the theosophists tread on common ground in Atlantis, that part of the theosophist theory which concerns the origin of the fifth Atlantean sub-race, the Semites, who came from the British Isles, then the Northern promontory of Atlantis, and were chosen by the Manu to be the founders of the Aryan Root Race. Blake was expressing a very similar notion when he wrote the famous lines

> And did those feet in ancient times
> Walk upon England's mountains green?
> And was the holy lamb of God
> On England's pleasant pastures seen?

Where did this idea come from?

Few people who sing Parry's setting of the hymn *Jerusalem* realize that after nearly 200 years they are feeling the pulse of the quaint erudition which in the 18th century plunged poets and parsons into scientific controversies about Biblical history and sowed the seeds of aggressive nationalism.

Two characteristic phases of 18th century thought unite in Blake's enormously confused cosmic and mythological system; the renaissance of interest in Atlantis and the craze for Celtic culture.[1] Nowadays, as T. S. Eliot has pointed out, Blake is too often regarded as a "wild pet for the super-cultivated" and enthusiastic Blakeists are apt to forget that

he was essentially a man of his times, nourished intellectually by the writings of rationalists and sceptics, the
scientific speculations of the learned academicians, and the
earnest and amateurish archaeological researches of eccen-
tric old country gentlemen. The connection between Blake's
symbolism and this background of period is often forgotten,
because he uses his symbols so intensely that they become
transmuted. His fierce honesty of purpose bombards with
complete success the unpromising heap of period oddities
that are incorporated haphazard into his cosmic system, and
releases the latent truth pent up in all experience. It is the
alchemy of genius to make inert matter give off energy in
the process of transmutation, and in this sense Blake belongs to all centuries. But it is to the 18th that he must
ultimately be related.

In 1706 appeared Pezron's *L'Antiquité de la Langue des
Celtes*, claiming a Celtic origin for Greek culture. This
book marked the beginning of a rising tide of Celtomania
which reached its high-water mark about the third quarter
of the century as a result of Stukeley's theories of the origin
of Stonehenge and Avebury, and then slowly ebbed again
to its low-water mark in the first quarter of the 19th century.
After that for a while the main tide passed underground
into occultist tradition, bubbling up now and then to serve
as material for Peacock's burlesques and to irrigate the vast
etymological system of Godfrey Higgins. By that time
Byron's poems and the taste of the Prince Regent had
established the more exotic craze for the orient.

The works of the Rev. William Stukeley were widely read in England and it is certain that Blake was influenced by them. Stukeley was the most famous and probably the best of the 18th century antiquaries. His work on Stonehenge and Avebury set a high standard of accurate observation in field archaeology and his careful notes and drawings have been of considerable value to later, more scientific investigators.[2] Unfortunately he was not content merely to observe and note. He began to construct theories of the origins of race and religion in order to explain the "antique stones," for despite his scientific training he was something of a mystic. In 1721, during his investigations of Avebury and Stonehenge, he became a freemason and about then he began to connect Stonehenge with the Druids. He built a druidical Grove and Temple in his own garden and soon he was convinced that the Druids were the forerunners of Christianity. Study of the pagan religions filled him with revivalist enthusiasm and he saw in his archaeological experience a powerful weapon against the "age of epidemical infidelity" in which he lived. To this end he embarked on what his friend Gale called his "theological enlargements" upon the archaeological work at Avebury. In his *Stonehenge, Temple Restored to the British Druids* (1740), he stated that the Druids who were of the patriarchal religion, which was the same as Christianity, came to England about the time of Abraham. They were an oriental colony, led by an Egyptian-Phoenician Hercules who built temples wherever he went. Migrating west, they settled among the first Celtic inhabitants of Europe. They built, of course, Stonehenge and Avebury, the latter upon an elaborate symbolical plan. "We have seen by our description that the plan upon which *Abury* is built, is the sacred hierogram of the *Egyptians*, and other ancient nations, the circle, snake, and wings. By this they meant to picture out, as well as they could, the nature of the divinity. The circle meant the supreme fountain of all being, the father; the serpent, that divine emanation from him which was called the son; the wings imported that other divine emanation from them which was called the spirit, the *anima mundi*." But though Stukeley concedes an eastern origin to the colony of Druids who built this symbolic masterpiece he is not lacking in patriotism. And this is where Atlantis, still a mere bud in the flowering garden of 18th century thought, comes in handy. "When we contemplate the elegance of this county of Wiltshire and the great works of antiquity therein, we may be persuaded that the two Atlantic islands and the Islands of the Blessed, which Plato and other ancient writers mention, were those *in reality* of *Britain* and *Ireland*."

A little later in the century Atlantis blossomed forth in the same herbaceous border as the Celtomania, and side by side they were cultivated, admired, and discussed by amateurs and connoisseurs alike.

Between 1775 and 1787 Jean Bailly, member of the Academy of Sciences, public servant, and later victim of the

French Revolution, was publishing his learned *Histoire de l'Astronomie*. In it he developed a grandiose system of racial migrations, based upon certain recurrent errors in astronomical tables brought back by some missionaries from India. Bailly, influenced by the theories of a Swedish savant called Olaus Rudbeck who had attempted to identify Atlantis with Upsala, maintained that the errors in the astronomical tables showed that they could not have been drawn up from observations made in India at all, but in Central Asia, at a latitude of 49°; the tables must have been evolved by a people who had migrated south from the polar or hyperborean continent and from whom all other races were derived. Plato's Atlantis was really Spitzbergen; and adopting Buffon's theory of a gradually cooling fire in the centre of the earth Bailly argued that Spitzbergen, once the warm and fertile land described by Plato in the *Critias*, in time grew so cold that the Atlanteans were forced south to Tartary.

This theory was popularised by Bailly's famous *Lettres sur les Origines des Sciences* and his *Lettres sur L'Atlantide* (1777). In fact it became so popular that in the north it assumed the quality of a legend and recent statements by Arctic explorers that there are warm fertile valleys tucked away in the polar regions[3] have given the legend a new lease of life. The letters were addressed to Voltaire and were received by the great man with scepticism but with the respect due to the author's literary ability and imaginative power. Books about Atlantis are apt to refer to this correspondence as though it were very acrimonious and academic, but in actual fact it was very charming and polite and full of nice inter-complimenting. "I assure you," wrote Voltaire in his fourth letter to Bailly, "that I have never read M. Mairan's theory of the internal heat of the earth compared with that produced by the heat of the summer sun. I was merely convinced that there is fire everywhere.

"Ignis ubique latet, naturam amplectitur omnem. The artichokes and asparagus we ate this January during a period of ice and snow, were grown without the help of a single ray of sunshine and without artificial heat, and are proof enough for me that the earth has a very strong intrinsic heat. But the contents of your ninth letter have given me a lot more information than the contents of my kitchen garden . . ."

But others attacked Bailly less gently. He had reckoned without the Celtomaniacs, whose object in life was to show that all civilization came from the west and were irritated to find that Bailly's theory was directly opposed to their ideas. It was a question of national honour as well as of science. "Dégrader ainsi nos ayeux," wrote the Abbé Baudeau in his *Mémoire à consulter pour les anciens Druids Gaulois contre M. Bailly, de l'académie des Sciences* . . . "dégrader ainsi nos ayeux et leurs philosophes, dans leur propre pays, à la face de leur postérité même, n'est-ce pas attenter en quelque forte à la gloire Nationale?"

By the end of the century the theory that those ancient Celtic Druids were of westerly origin was the mainstay of the Welsh Nationalists. Books like Edward Williams'

Welsh Poems (1794) and Edward Davies' *Celtic Researches* (1804) started a craze for Bards and Pitries. Britain was the abode of the Pitries, fathers of the human race. The deluge drowned all mankind except two, who escaped to Britain in a boat and re-peopled the island after the flood had subsided. Religion was brought from the west by the Druids, originators of all civilization, science and learning, especially the Jewish.

These were the creamy notions which Blake lapped up. The conception of Atlantis as the western paradise from which these patriarchs escaped to Britain after the deluge was not properly fixed until the full occultist legend of Fabre d'Olivet, the celebrated orientalist mystic who is said to have proposed to Napoleon that he should form a European Empire with himself as its spiritual head,[4] was given to the world in his *Histoire Philosophique du Genre Humain* (1827). But it is probable that already by the end of the century the tradition was formed orally in the Swedenborgian and Occultist circles frequented by Blake.[5]

At any rate Blake took advantage of the plastic state of the Atlantis story to mould it into a form which could help him to express his subjective truths, and in his hands it became a powerful symbol. But one looks in vain for any explicit general statement of his Atlantean credo. It has to be inferred from a number of scattered allusions, the meaning which was plain to the public for whom Blake wrote. Piecing these allusions together, we find that Atlantis was between Britain and America (p. 222. *Nonesuch Blake*), or perhaps Britain itself was actually a remnant of the lost continent (p. 618). When it sank, Albion, patriarch of the Atlantic, came to Britain; he became the parent of the Druids among whom were Abraham, Shem, and Noah (pp. 597, 797), "as the Patriarchal pillars and Oak Groves all over the world bear witness to this day."

"All things begin and end in Albion's ancient rocky Druid shore."

"Britain was the primitive seat of the patriarchal religion, and Jerusalem was and is the emanation of the Giant Albion."

"London walked in every nation, mutual in love and
  harmony
"Albion covered the whole earth, England encompasses
  the Nations
"Mutual each within other's bosom in visions of regener-
  ation.
"Jerusalem covered the Atlantic mountains and the
  Erythean
"From bright Japan and China to Hesperia, France and
  England."

At the Fall, Jerusalem was separated from England; at the Reconstitution it will return and the twelve tribes of Israel shall be settled in the English counties, according to Blake's scheme for allotting them. The Fall meant disintegration and despair.

> Jerusalem fell from Lambeth's vale
> Down through Poplar and Old Bow,
> Through Maldon and across the Sea
> In war and howling, death and woe.

But out of this vision of despair grows Blake's message of personal determination and hope:

> I shall not cease from mental fight
> Nor shall my sword sleep in my hand
> Till we have built Jerusalem
> In England's green and pleasant land.

For Blake this identification of England–Atlantis and Jerusalem was a visual reality as well as a symbolic way of expressing in condensed form the idea that the builders of Jerusalem were Druids who had migrated from England after the fall of Man, and shall one day return. He loved England, Golden Square as well as the cottage at Felpham with its "thatched roof of rusted gold." England was real to him because he lived there. But he also loved his golden Jerusalem, which was no less real to him because he imagined it. And so, with that astonishing double vision which had enabled him as a child to *see* a group of angels in a tree in Peckham Rye, he again saw the dream and the reality in one vision:

> The fields from Islington to Marylebone,
> To Primrose Hill and Saint John's Wood
> Were builded over with pillars of Gold
> And there Jerusalem's pillars stood.

From this point of view his treatment of the Atlantis–Albion-Jerusalem myth is unique and is characteristic of his peculiarly symbolic way of writing poetry. But it is interesting to find that in the main his conception of the myth is similar to that of all Atlantomaniacs before and since; and here, aside from poetry or mysticism, we have a heaven-sent opportunity to study Atlantis in relation to the common desires of the individual; for Blake does not react to the germ of Atlantomania in any *abnormal* way, but ten times more strongly than the normal individual, a difference of degree and not of kind.

(2)

Blake's conception of Atlantis is in no way extraordinary for an imaginative and sensitive Englishman living in the 18th century and there is much in it which may be interpreted in terms of common human experience to-day. For Blake, as for other rebels like Shelley and D. H. Lawrence, Freedom is almost an obsession. In his rage against society, his inability to fit his philosophy into any recognized system, his ceaseless ranging over great tracts of space and time, all loosed in epic outpourings of undisciplined verse, one has the feeling of a Titan spirit chained down to a pigmy body which is domiciled in Lambeth and prevented from achieving expression by an inadequate intellect and the limitations of language. In Blake's theory all culture and religion comes from Albion and therefore England covers the earth at all stages of history; hence the earth is the heritage of the English who are free to wander all over it—an idea, in the opinion of foreigners, common among imperially minded Englishmen even to-day! But Blake finds that in practice his mystical empire is disrupted, both spiritually and territorially, and he himself, pent up in Albion's ancient rocky Druid shore, feels a kind of claustrophobia. He is

223

particularly attracted towards the wide open spaces of America, not long before become independent, and there are many references to "Canadian wilds," "the soft American plains," "my American plains," connected in his mind with the lost land-bridge which once made it possible for Englishmen to reach America across

> Those vast shady hills between America and Albion's shore
> Now barred out by the Atlantic Ocean, called Atlantean hills . . .

In those primaeval days, Blake seems to imply, Albion and America were a territorial as well as a spiritual unit, Atlantis. But now the ocean divides and imprisons, falsifying his dream, based upon his conception of the facts of prehistory, of a union of the English speaking peoples, not so very different from the dreams of many people to-day.

> Enslaved the Daughters of Albion weep, a trembling lamentation
> Upon their mountains; in their valleys, sigh towards America.

The lines echo the nostalgia of the Jews in captivity.

> By the waters of Babylon, there we sat down, yea, we wept when we remembered Zion.

This deep principle of unity among the nations, which exists in Blake side by side with his English nationalism, is the obverse side of the longing to be free and is based upon the appeal to origins, to the primitive Albion, compact heir of the Titan Atlanteans from whom all peoples and their works are emanations. And here, in the tangle of Blake's thought, the question of sexual unity is also involved, for Albion is a divine hermaphrodite. His conception of the universal brotherhood of Man through the Division of the One (Jesus, Albion, or Adam) is in the main tradition of occultist thought and he is merely echoing the doctrine believed in his family and accepted in occultist circles at the time. But in his conception of the Reconstitution of the One, a process which begins with the regeneration of passion, he is dealing with a personal problem in the light of his own mystical experience. The longing to escape from personality with all its inevitable accompanying sense of loneliness by passionate self-forgetting union with other human beings has never been more grandly expressed than in the *Prelude* to *America*. In it the world is saved by the nuptial union of Orc and Vale, the Shadowy Daughter of Orthona, who cries:

> I know thee, I have found thee, and I will not let thee go
> Thou art the image of God who dwells in the darkness of
>   Africa,
> And thou art fallen to give me life in regions of dark
>   death . . .

This was the much-misunderstood solution of D. H. Lawrence, bearing an obvious message for post-war Europeans whose desire to throw off the burden of lonely individuality has been greatly increased by the new self-consciousness produced by discoveries in psychology. Both prophets turn to the "dark gods" of sense, and both look back to the primitive peoples for the secret of the true way of life. For Blake, caught up on the cresting wave of Celtic Nationalism, it was the Druids who brought the message to England, and he believes that it still survived among naked heroes in the Welsh mountains.

"In the meantime," he wrote, in the descriptive catalogue of his paintings, "he (Mr Blake) has painted this picture which supposes that in the reign of the British Prince, who lived in the 5th century (Arthur), there were remains of those naked Heroes in the Welsh Mountains; they are there now, Gray saw them in the person of his bard on Snowdon; there they dwell in naked simplicity; happy is he who can see and converse with them above the shadows of generations and death."

The same thought is expressed in the introduction to the *Songs of Experience*:

> Hear the voice of the Bard
> Who Present, Past and Future, sees;
> Whose ears have heard
> The holy word
> That walked among the ancient trees.

For Lawrence, too, trees had associations with the Word, or, in Lawrence's very different idiom, the "delicate magic" which has gone from life.

> Folded in like a dark thought
> Of which the language is lost
> Tuscan cypresses,
> Is there a great secret?
> Are our words no good?

Vast Shady Hills

The undeliverable secret,
Dead with a dead race and a dead speech, and yet
Darkly monumental in you, Etruscan cypresses.
Ah how I admired your fidelity
Dark cypresses.

Is it the secret of the long-nosed Etruscans?
The long-nosed, sensitive-footed, subtly-smiling
    Etruscans
Who made so little noise outside the cypress groves?

He says nothing of the Lost Atlantis, but he is unconsciously a good Atlantean mystic in his passionate belief that the primitive was the essential, that those forgotten ancient peoples were initiated into the "delicate magic" now lost to the world.

In the *Plumed Serpent* it is Quexacoatl, the God of the Aztecs, who guards the secret of the ancient people. Only by reviving his cult can the Mexicans recover the spirit of the "old prehistoric humanity, the dark-eyed humanity of the days, perhaps, before the glacial period. When the world was colder, and the seas emptier, and all the land-formation was different. When the waters of the world were piled in stupendous glaciers on the high places, and high, high, upon the poles. When the great plains stretched away to the oceans, like Atlantis and the lost continents of Polynesia, so that seas were only great lakes, and the soft, dark-eyed people of that world could walk round the globe. Then there was a mysterious, hot-blooded, soft-footed humanity with a strange civilization of its own."

The word "lost " is indeed the keynote of all Atlantean

227

mysticism; it is full of the pain of longing for the unattainable and yet contains the irrepressible hope which refuses to recognize the destructability of beautiful things; for if the substantial forms of beauty pass beyond human perception, their shadow may still be felt lurking in the folds of dark secrets.

But many do not feel the need to pry into secret things; for them lost beauties are imminent throughout nature, in the clear daylight as well as by night. This idea is finely expressed in John Masefield's *Fragments*. Mr Masefield imagines the Atlanteans much as the Occultists and Mystics do. They are wiser and more sensitive than we are. They are pale-faced and hushed like Lawrence's Etruscans, and they wander softly about their proud courts to the tune of lovely thoughts which sing like birds within their chambers.

> They knew all wisdom, for they knew
> The souls of the Egyptian Kings
> Who learnt, in ancient Babilu,
> The beauty of immortal things.

That is really a poetization of all that Rudolph Steiner tells us about the minds of the Atlanteans.

Then came the deluge, and the greedy sea washed over their golden courts. Now the shadowy coral grows among them and the sharks haunt the hidden ways of the sunken city.

> But, at the falling of the tide,
> The golden birds still sing and gleam,
> The Atlanteans have not died,
> Immortal things still give us dream.

Vast Shady Hills

The dream that fires man's heart to make,
To build, to do, to sing and say,
A beauty death can never take,
An Adam from the crumbled clay.

This dream is the common experience of both poets and occultists. An illusion, perhaps, but a cherished one.

LOST DREAMS AND PLAINTIVE HOPES

"Weeping down somewhere in the Atlantic the day's great eye leaves a gauzy gold-haze above black woods. Sentiment long since honoured the West with lost dreams and plaintive hopes. Can I believe I was myself so late out there on a burning sea, within that sunset magic and treading its elfin gold? Where has that sun gone? Isles of the Blest, Atlantis?"

Atlantic Crossing. G. WILSON KNIGHT.

(1)

If we trace the history of the Atlantis legend from Plato to modern times we discover the surprising fact that it has almost always been regarded as a geological or poetic theme and not as a moral tragedy. The framework of the Platonic dialogues is usually forgotten in the excitement created by the legend of a lost continent, which appeals so strongly to the popular imagination that it has been considered pedantry to examine it in relation to its source in Plato's philosophy. Honesty, however, demands that this should be done.

The clue to an understanding of the relationship of the legend to its source is contained in the account of the ancient Hellenes in the *Critias*. This is actually a very rough sketch of the first five books of the *Republic*, and was probably intended by Plato to remind his readers of the whole of the earlier work, with which he would expect them to be already familiar. But there is a great deal more of the Atlantis story which seems to be derived from the same source, and we can see how Plato, re-reading his *Republic* after a lapse of years, might have conceived the idea of adapting a ready made story about a sunk Atlantic continent as a popular illustration of his theories; which suggests that Plato's contemporaries and followers, with the master's writings and reputation fresh in their memory, probably interpreted the story as an allegory. That at any rate seems to be the most fruitful, though by no means the only, construction to put upon it.

On the mythological plane the *Timaeus* and *Critias* give us the conflict of two races, one of which represents the civilized world of the Greeks and the other a barbarian civilization from the back of beyond. The former is a Utopian fixation of society according to Plato's ideal, the latter an exaggerated illustration of what might happen in a real state exposed to the temptation of natural abundance and the inevitable process of decay. "Since everything that has come into being must one day perish, even a system like ours (the perfect state of aristocracy) will not endure for all time, but must suffer dissolution." (*Republic* VIII, 546).[1] After the dissolution of the good state or Aristocracy, a society passes through four stages of progressive decadence which Plato calls Timocracy, Oligarchy, Democracy and Despotism, each of which is less "just" than the predecessor. The chief characteristics of this decadence, which results in the first place from the degeneration of the ruling

231

class (546) are ambition, love of gold and silver, a warlike spirit and licentiousness; but the most important aspect of it is the money-getting instinct, which divides the state into rich and poor and breeds hate and revolution (555). "These capitalists . . . keep prying after their own interests, and apparently do not see their enemies; and whenever one of the remainder yields them opportunity, they wound him by infusing their poisonous money, and then recover interest many times as great as the parent sum, and thus make the drone and the beggar multiply in the state." This was precisely what happened to the Atlanteans who caught the infection of "covetousness and pride of power"; and their capitalist society, which sums up the four stages of decay after the break-up of an aristocracy in the Republic, contrasts with the small town socialism of the ideal state.

Again, psychologically interpreted, the Greek-Atlantean opposition may be compared to different states in the soul of one man. These are the rational and appetitive principles which Plato (*Republic* Bk. IV) describes as contradictory impulses proceeding from the same source, and tries, not very convincingly, to correlate with the ruling and productive classes in the state. Thus the Greek state corresponds to the rational self-controlling function of the intellect and the rich imperialistic Atlanteans to that part of the soul "with which it loves and hungers and thirsts and experiences the flutter of the other desires." This is called the "irrational and concupiscent principle, the ally of sundry indulgences and pleasures." In the same way Plato's thesis that the rational and concupiscent principles proceed from one source is represented in the *Timaeus* and *Critias* by the fact that the rival civilizations of Greece and Atlantis, which at first sight appear to be entirely opposed to one another, actually inter-penetrate a good deal. Life both in Athens and Atlantis is highly organized and regimented; both delight in technical works and sciences, and specialization is a common feature. Neither, to begin with at any rate, are touched by the evils of economic competition. Fundamentally Atlantis is just as ideal as Athens; it only ceases to be ideal when its inhabitants, with the weakening of the divine strain in them wake up to the possibilities of exploiting their natural wealth for selfish ends.

In various degrees these oppositions are all implicit in the full story of Atlantis. To what extent Plato intended them to be there is irrelevant. And though no single interpretation taken by itself is really fruitful, taken together and related to the supposed facts underlying the composition of the dialogues they give us a much more significant story than we might suppose. But the chief value of the interpretive process is that it shows the necessity to distinguish between Atlantis, the Platonic *myth* and Atlantis the *legend* which is incorporated in the myth.

Atlantis, the legend of the geologists and poets, is much simpler than the myth. Shorn of all tragic significance and detached from its mythological setting it emerges into history as a tale of a marvellous city on a fertile western island sunk beneath the ocean in a great cataclysm. This

233

poetic legend immediately becomes speculatively important as part of the problem of the origins and distribution of
life. Our attitude towards the process depends of course
upon whether we believe that there was a tradition before
Plato. If we believe that Plato invented the story, then we
must admit that the geological and poetical Atlantis has
"nothing to do with the case;" generations of Atlantophils
would have done better to read their Plato more carefully
before starting on a wild goose chase. If, on the other hand,
we believe in the essential truth of the story, that Plato's
version of it lost touch with the reality it represented, then
we may regard the legend which has abided the question
of enquiring minds for more then 2,000 years as a return
to the essential Atlantis that the world knew about before
Plato wrote his *Timaeus* and *Critias*. But whatever attitude
we adopt, the fact that Atlantis did emerge from its mythological setting as a full-fledged geological mystery and not
as a moral tragedy has been largely responsible for the long
lease of life it has enjoyed and will probably continue to
enjoy indefinitely.

(2)

The detached and simplified legend that has been transmitted chiefly by speculative scientists, romance writers
and, very rarely, by non-Christian moralists in search of a
substitute for the Biblical flood, has a certain anthropological interest. For within limits it can be regarded as a
test case for determining different stages in the development of western thought.

234

Lost Dreams and Plaintive Hopes

In the 6th century A.D., the Atlantis conceived by the Byzantine geographer Cosmas Indicapleustes is a sign-post to the intellectual situation created by the adoption of Christianity as the official religion of the Roman Empire. One important effect of Christian authority was to suppress the cosmographical theories of the classical scientists and in particular the belief, generally accepted by educated persons in classical times, that the earth is spherical. Even in the classical period there had always been a popular conception of the earth as being flat, surviving from the earliest times. And when Christianity was faced with the necessity of making a ruling on this question, it was found that the doctrine of the earth's flatness squared much better with the Scriptures than that of its roundness, which savoured of pagan science. In Cosmas this flatness theory is pushed to its extreme, and although his work has been described as a "monument of unconscious humour"[2] it is symptomatic not only of the fluid state of early Christian doctrine but also of the age-old conflict between science and religion which found its most typical expression 1,000 years later in Gallileo's quarrel with the Inquisition.

Cosmas, himself tainted with Nestorian heresy, vigorously denounced the doctrine of the sphericity of the earth as heretical. He maintained that the earth was a rectangle twice as broad as it was long, like the table of the shewbread; that the earth was two-storied, the upper storey contained the angels, and that the sun revolved round a great mountain in the north, hiding itself behind it at night. The known world he conceived as an island surrounded on all sides by a huge ocean which was itself encompassed by an outer continent. To prove the existence of this exterior continent he invoked Atlantis as described by Plato in the *Timaeus*, but he contended that Plato was mistaken in placing Atlantis in the west and separating it from the exterior continent. This error was due to a misinterpretation of the primitive traditions kept by Moses, which showed that Atlantis was really the eastern part of the outer continent. Plato's history of Atlantean man, however, was accepted by Cosmas as the true story of antediluvian civilization, the ten kings of Atlantis representing the ten generations from Adam to Noah!

For many centuries after Cosmas, Atlantis lay buried in the Dark Ages. But the legend survived in the translations of Arab scholars who handed it on to the early mediaeval precursors of the Age of Discovery.

In the 14th century the amazing voyages of the Portuguese seamen stimulated the rest of Europe with the spirit of adventure and the desire to conquer new lands. The same urge which had once drawn the Phoenician ships beyond the Pillars of Hercules in search of metals now caused the British and Portuguese to risk their lives in search of the fabulous wealth of the Indies. At this time sea exploration was particularly attractive because of the renewed interest in the theories of the Greek and Latin cosmographers, who, on the assumption that the earth was spherical, had calculated from an estimate of the area of the known world that it was possible to reach the Indies by a westerly passage. These theories had been more or less current since the 13th century when the speculative monk Roger Bacon had endorsed Aristotle's opinion that "the sea is small between the end of Spain on the west and the beginning of the Indies on the east," and Seneca's statement that with a favourable wind this western sea could be navigated in a few days' sailing. Further hopes were aroused by a study of the *Timaeus*, and after the discovery and colonization of the Azores by the Portuguese, the imagination of cosmographers soon placed other islands upon their maps, Brazil, Antillia, St. Brandon's Isle, the Fortunate Islands and many others, including Atlantis itself, despite its legendary disappearance. The Atlantis of the 15th century map-makers is a symbol of the great period of romantic geography which led to the discovery of America.

But after the discovery of America the ghost of Atlantis was laid to the satisfaction of most of the authoritative geographers. Atlantis-America became no more than an incidental factor in the search for the north-west passage to Cathay. During the 16th century Atlantis became less and less interesting as a romantic objective until at the beginning of the 17th century Francis Bacon's *New Atlantis* marks the beginning of the new scientific spirit of the age which produced Sir Thomas Browne and the Royal Society, intolerant of "vulgar errors" and determined to undertake the study of nature seriously. Bacon's conception of the historical

237

truth underlying the legend of Atlantis (see p. 108) thus prepares the way for the popular scientific speculations of the 18th century, typified by the interest taken in Atlantis by such different minds as Stukeley, Voltaire and Blake. Nationalism and religion begin to exploit the half-baked theories of pseudo-scientists in the general appeal to the origins of civilization. At this time more than any other the tendency to regard Atlantis as a means to an end rather than an end in itself becomes apparent, though Blake, influenced by the strain of romanticism as well as the rationalism in 18th century thought, shows that the lost continent theme has an intrinsic appeal to the imagination.

Blake's Atlantean primitivism, though esoteric in character, is really only an exaggeration of the romantic philosophy of Rousseau which had such a tremendous effect upon the thought of his century. To some extent it was the result of a natural revolt from the restraining influences of 18th century classicism. "The exaltation of the primitive ages," says Professor Irving Babbitt, "is simply the projection into a mythical past of the need that the man of the 18th century feels to let himself go." During the last thirty years of Blake's life this somewhat narrow romanticism, which had characterized the Ossianic poems, developed into the full naturalistic philosophy associated with the "romantics," Wordsworth, Coleridge, Keats, Shelley and Byron. The tremendous popularity and wide circulation of Byron's Childe Harold helped to spread the ideal of the "noble savage" throughout Europe and in 1814 the Scottish novelist John Galt, who travelled with Byron from Gibraltar to Malta and afterwards wrote a biography of him, published a typically Rousseauistic tragedy called *The Apostate, or Atlantis Destroyed*. "The train of moral sentiment in the piece," wrote Galt, who included it as an anonymous contribution to a volume of original dramas collected and edited by himself, "is evidently derived from Rousseau's celebrated essay against the arts and sciences."

Yamos, king and founder of Atlantis, has been converted to Christianity and induced to adopt the arts and sciences of Europe by the persuading tongue of Antonio, survivor of a shipwreck on the coasts of Atlantis. The king has implicit faith in Antonio, although Antonio is busily trying to seduce his Queen. The high priest of the ancient religion, who has been forced by the King's apostasy to flee to the forest accompanied by a little band of devoted pagans, returns one day to the court and remonstrates with his royal master:

> O swift retrace your steps
> To that simplicity that once was yours,
> Already lo your new-found arts require
> Inventions to remind you of the God.

Later the high priest has a spirited interview with Antonio himself, who is represented as a rather attractive serpent-in-the-Garden-of-Eden. "You taught us arts," shouts the high priest—

> Divided us in bands
> These for the chace and these to seed the soil,
> And when your tongue had learnt our simple speech,

You spoke of life and worlds beyond the stars,
And called our ancient rites of gratitude
To the great Spirit—aimless superstition.

Antonio:
In doing so I know that I did well.

Orooko:
The proof of that must show in the effect.
But I proceed—dissensions rose among us—
Your altars prospered, while with hapless me
A few undaunted faithful chose the woods.
Here, here, enchanted by your seeming wisdom,
Thousands on thousands swarmed to raise the
town.
And it was raised. For this eternal temple,
High in whose measureless concave the sun,
A lamp of everlasting splendor shines,
You have th' Apostates from their father's God,
Led to a mansion built by their own hands,
And made them kneel before such feeble
emblems
As the soft-breathing of a bird might
quench . . .

Galt did not believe in Atlantis and therefore his Eden is
less convincing primitivism than Blake's abode of naked
heroes, but on the whole his *Atlantis Destroyed* is an excellent illustration of the relation of the romantic conception
of man's Fall from Nature to man's Fall from God in the
Christian theology. And Galt also has his romantic equivalent of the Flood, for in the last act of the tragedy Antonio
and the adulterous queen are brought to book, and the
wicked city of Atlantis, the urban hell which is threatening
the pastoral heaven of Atlantean life, is burnt to the ground.

But the important point to notice is that it is destroyed by the Atlanteans themselves; urged on by the high priest they hurl firebrands into their city and burn it to ashes. Thus Galt, true to Rousseau, concedes nothing to the old theology and gives his audience no opportunity to ascribe the downfall of the city to Fate or the Hand of God. Galt's play is one of the few historical examples of a moral interpretation of the Atlantis theme, and as such it has greater anthropological value than the purely geological or Arcadian interpretations because it is shown as a typical product of 18th–19th century thinking.

One April, fifty years after the publication of *Atlantis Destroyed*, John Ruskin, influential dilettante, went to lecture to the citizens of Bradford, who were about to spend £30,000 on building an Exchange, on good taste in architecture. His lecture was more like a sermon . . . [3]

In 1859, Ruskin had toured the north and had been profoundly shocked by the change in the countryside which had been brought about by the industrial revolution. Everywhere the green fields were being defiled by "dark satanic mills" and squalid factories, and the conditions of the working class were appalling. How could such a civilization, he asked himself, hope to produce beautiful things? And since the fostering of works of true art was his mission in life he decided that he must henceforth dedicate himself to the improvement of the moral health of the people who permitted such monstrous eyesores to deface the country in the name of Business.

To this end he reminded his audience of astonished manufacturers, who had invited the famous lecturer to come and talk to them about architecture, of the wisdom of a certain pagan, Plato, and of the circumstances which led to the destruction of the rich commercial city of Atlantis. He accused them of setting up an idol of riches like the decadent Atlanteans. "This idol of yours," he thundered, "this golden image high by measureless cubits, set up where your green fields of England are furnace-burnt into the likeness of the plain of Dura . . . if you continue to make that forbidden deity your principal one, soon no more art, no more science, no more pleasure will be possible. Catastrophe will come; or, worse than catastrophe, slow mouldering and withering in Hades."

Ruskin's interpretation of the Atlantis theme, though superficially similar to Galt's at the beginning of the century is actually very different. Aside from his individual eccentricities Ruskin is in many ways a typical product of mid-Victorian England and his conception of Atlantis is characteristic. Galt's play represented the Pagan naturalism of an age which was still kicking itself free from century old traces and Galt speaks in the voice of a rebel. Ruskin stands for Christian discipline in a period of intellectual freedom and he preaches like an evangelist. He revels in Turneresque sunsets and rolling hills, but he sees human life with the pietistic unimaginative eye of a nonconformist ascetic. And though in his championship of the Pre-Raphaelite painters, he did not associate himself with their sickly tendency towards mediaevalism, his pious misunderstanding of the true nature of Gothic is characteristic of the uncertain values, both moral and aesthetic, of many mid-Victorians reacting to the impact of Mills' *Liberty* and Darwin's *Origin of the Species.* Ruskin's sincere but somewhat complicated and quaintly emphasized rendering of the final passage in the *Critias* is full of the spirit of Queen Victoria's England.

"Through many generations, so long as the God's nature in them yet was full, they were submissive to the sacred laws, and carried themselves lovingly to all that had kindred with them in divineness; for their uttermost spirit was faithful and true, and in every wise great; so that *in all meekness of wisdom, they dealt with each other*, and so took all the chances of life; and despising all things except virtue, they cared little what happened day by day, and *bore lightly the burden* of gold and possessions ; for they saw that, if only *their common love and virtue increased, all these things would be increased together with them;* but to set their esteem and ardent pursuit upon material possession would be to lose that first, and their virtue and affection together with it. And by such reasoning and what of the divine nature remained in them, they gained all this greatness of which we have already told; but when the God's part in them faded and became extinct, being mixed again and again, and effaced by the prevalent mortality; and the human nature at last exceeded, they then became unable to endure the course

243

of nature; and fell into shapelessness of life, and baseness
in the sight of Him who could see, having lost everything
that was fairest of their honour, while to the blind hearts,
which could not discern the true life tending to happiness,
it seemed that they were then chiefly noble and happy,
being filled with all iniquity of inordinate possessions and
power. Whereupon the God of Gods, whose kinghood is in
laws, beholding a once just nation thus cast into misery
and desirous to lay such punishment upon them as might
make them repent into restraining, gathered together all the
gods into His dwelling place, which from heaven's centre
overlooks whatever has part in creation; and having
assembled them, He said . . ."

(3)

What significance, if any, has the Atlantis theme for
the present day? In a civilization which is primarily concerned with the problem of preserving itself from being
destroyed in war, is it worth bothering about a sunken
continent?

Once again it is necessary to distinguish between Plato's
Atlantis and the legend of Atlantis which has become
popular through centuries of geological speculation. The
latter, it seems, can hardly be of much value to those who
really know the state of responsible scientific opinion on the
problem; and it can only be of vital interest for people who
have so lost faith in progress that they are ready to accept

any ready made dream to provide them with an escape from the dust and rattle of machine-governed existence. As the home of original good Atlantis is frankly a sham, haunted by the pale ghost of romantic primitivism that lingers on despite the change in values since the industrial revolution.

> Now our research is done, measured the shadow,[4]
> The hills mapped out, the hills a natural boundary.
> Such and such is our country. There remains
> To plough up the meadowland, reclaim the marshes.

This is true in the sense that now is the time to consolidate the "progress" of invention and discovery during the last hundred years, to learn how to use the resources of the newly-conquered country; for at the moment many people are so perplexed by the breakdown of reason, the disease of over-production and the intellectual frustration involved in the attempt to find an honest compromise between the conflicting claims of Science and Religion as arbiters of ethics, that they would evacuate the country which has cost so much to conquer. But there can be no return to the past.

> It will be useless! Only machines reverse.[5]
> All that has mind may not go arseverse.

We are now concerned with the past more as a means of understanding the present than as an end in itself. The Lost Atlantis, if ever it can be fitted into the scheme of history, may prove to be of great importance. But until scientific progress settles the question one way or the other, serious speculations are idle.

But the Platonic myth has a permanent significance, and to-day more than ever it can profitably be re-read as one of the great products of the romantic imagination. It sounds paradoxical to apply the term romantic to a product of a classical period like the 5th–3rd century B.C. in Greece; but the use of the term is easily justifiable and the point is important.

A common characteristic of romantic writing is that it is symbolical. Words seem to imply more than they say and the meaning overflows the form. This is true of Plato's description of Atlantis in the *Critias*, which also in its general outline suggests romantic "vision," that appreciation of the infinite that can only be created by expense of spirit. Everything about Atlantis is rich and strange, anticipating what is surely the greatest of all romances, *The Tempest*. Both Shakespeare and Plato aim at novelty, and although Shakespeare's island seems more "visionary" because it is described in less detail than Plato's, the exotic character which he manages to give it by references to magic and the Indies, exactly corresponds to the effect produced by Plato's barbaric architecture and the strange religious rites of the Atlantean kings. And the reason for creating this exotic setting is not, as in purely Arcadian romances of the Kubla Khan order, to escape from life's problems, but to clarify them. Plato sails to Atlantis, not to escape from Athenian democracy but to find out what his ideal state is really like, to test by imaginative projection the conception of the true and the good upon which his

Republic is founded. L. H. Myers has made this point in the preface to his romantic novel *The Root and the Flower*. "And now I want to explain why I have chosen as my scene India at the end of the 16th century. My object has been to carry the reader away from the machinery of life that is familiar to him, to avoid the mention of names of places that hold associations that are foreign to my purpose, to obtain an attention undistracted by the social and economic problems of to-day. I am aware, however, that it is dangerous to fly too far. The storyteller who soars out of our earthly geography and history altogether starts with too great an emptiness before him. He has to tell you everything from the beginning; it cannot be taken for granted that in his superlunary world the sky is still blue, the grass still green." This is surely the *raison d'être* of exoticism in all romances which have a message, as genuine romances have. That is why Plato chose Atlantis as a testing ground for the validity of his preconceived ethics.

We know the result of his excursion into romance. It did not end like Shakespeare's to the sound of music, and the jagged edge of the *Critias* symbolizes both his personal failure to achieve what he had set out to do, and his inability to reconcile his discovery of the tragic destiny of the Atlanteans with his duty to the Gods. But the great value of the Atlantis myth as a romance is that it is honest. Professor Grierson has called Plato the first great romantic, but it would have been truer to give that title to Homer and describe Plato as the first *responsible* romantic.

To-day when those who write from a non-Christian point of view tend either towards a sterile neo-classicism based on the shifting sands of scientific fact, or else to an emotional romanticism which out-Rousseaus Rousseau in the bewildered effort to provide an adequate substitute for religion, there is a great deal to be said for disciplined romanticism, for an imaginative interpretation of facts in the light of some higher reality, the nature of which depends on subjective experience.

In the final estimate the myth of Atlantis stands as the classic example of spiritual adventure, of the Elizabethan imagination which sets sail to discover new and valuable attitudes to life, those remote Bermudas in the mind

> that ocean where each kind
> Does straight its own resemblance find.

In this sense, at any rate, the Lost Atlantis may yet be recovered from the depths of the ocean which engulfed it.

Appendix A

The following story, sent to the author by the owner of the house in question, may be of interest as a footnote to the chapter on the occultist theory of Atlantis, especially that part of it which deals with the White migrations from Atlantis during the period of Black ascendancy.

Towards the end of 1927 my husband and I took a long lease on an old early 14th century house in Kent. It was a rambling place with unexpected corners and full of very fine oak. One day, prior to moving in, I remarked to our landlord that such a place suggested ghosts and he laughingly replied that it had the reputation of being haunted by a sobbing lady in one of the bedrooms and an old man with a skull cap who was supposed to walk across the large beamed living room.

With his remarks in mind I later asked the chauffeur and charwoman (both local people) if they had heard it was haunted, and they both replied in the affirmative, but would not say what the ghost was supposed to be, though the woman said: "I wouldn't stay alone in that house for anything!"

It set me wondering whether, during the 600 years since it was built, there were any supernatural influences which had attached themselves to the place, and these thoughts were rather enhanced when my husband (a complete sceptic) remarked that he did not like our bedroom and felt uncomfortable in it "as though something walked through it."

This made me decide to have the house "cleared" of any possible spectral evidences that might be hanging about. Having heard of two men in town who were famous for having exorcized many well known places in various parts of the country, I wrote and asked them if they would drive down to inspect the place—rather to the amused annoyance of my husband who, by this time, said that the odd "feeling" he had had about our room was due to its size and the rather ominous curved oak beam which ran across the ceiling to support the king pin in the roof.

In due time the men came for the day and went over the house, systematically, from room to room. At one point, facing a wall not far from the entrance to our bedroom, they pointed to it and said: "Is there any water in that direction? Whatever it is comes through here, goes through your room out through your son's and describes a circle." I said there was a small pond outside the garden, in the meadow. We went to it. Here, after a few seconds, one of the men said: "There it is," and described to his companion an animal which he called a meru. I have forgotten the actual description, but I believe it was said to have the body of a bear and head of a wolf with a seal or insignia on its forehead. They then explained that this was a form of elemental, magically created by some Atlanteans ages and ages ago; that these

Atlanteans were fleeing from the evil which was overpower-
ing and ruining their continent and had set up camp on
this spot. Wishing to be protected during their sojourn, they
had created the meru (a benign influence) and had prescribed a circle round which it was to go until it was
disintegrated by them. There was evidence that the camp
had been struck and the refugees passed on, forgetting to
release their elemental protector which was still guarding
its circle—and it was the presence of the meru which my
husband had felt. The men suggested that nothing should
be done to disintegrate it since the influence was a good one
and as far as I know it is still here, though it no longers
walks through our room because they altered its course to
include the protection of the gardens as well.

It may be of interest to state here that we are in the
Kentish Weald, and *The Secret Doctrine*, vol. II, 348 states:
"The great English fresh-water deposit called the Wealden
—which every geologist regards as the mouth of a former
great river—*is the bed of the main stream which drained
Northern Lemuria in the Secondary age.*" (Italics theirs).

This being so, the Atlanteans of our story may, perhaps,
have escaped by boat to this spot.

Appendix B

ATLANTIS AND GLACIAL COSMOGONY

Quite a literature has gathered round the theory which dates from the publication in 1913 of Hoerbiger's *Glacial-Cosmogonie*. Its teachings are completely opposed to the current cosmogony and selenology, and its validity is denied by astronomers, who in general ignore it. This is why it has not been included in the main discussion of Atlantean theories, all of which accept the current cosmogony.

The only English account of the Cosmic Ice theory and its relation to the Atlantis theory is H. S. Bellamy's *Moons, Myths, and Man* (Faber 1936). The author presents it as a fruitful basis for the interpretation of the class of myths generally known as "cosmic," which are to be considered as faithful reports of the events which took place "at the beginning of things." This class comprises, "all the deluge and destruction myths, accounts of the creation of the Universe, the Earth, the Gods and Man; the descriptions of lost lands and forgotten arts; the tales of dragons and other monsters." To suit this conception all the basic principles of current mythology and geology require readjustment. Whether sound or unsound, the fundamental teaching and the mythological deductions it inspires outdo the wildest imaginings of the storytellers. Mythology fits it like a glove

. . . or perhaps the Cosmic Ice theory is the glove that fits the mythology.

Broadly and very simply the Cosmic Ice theory teaches that the inter-stellar spaces of the universe are not just ether, but are filled with extremely rarefied hydrogen which offers a slight but appreciable resistance to all bodies moving in it. The cosmic building materials are metals, chiefly iron and nickel, and gases, chiefly hydrogen and oxygen. Hydrogen is both free and combined with oxygen in its cosmic form, ice; oxygen, when liberated by heat from its compound, forms water, acts as fuel for star-matter and generates more heat. The chief motive forces of the universe are gravity and steam explosion, the former collective and the latter distributive; there are also "inertia" forces, new tensions created by the resistance of the inter-stellar medium. This resistance causes all bodies moving in it in a "straight line" to slow up and eventually to stop all bodies moving in orbits to round out and decrease those orbits, so that they approach their mass centres in fine spirals and finally unite with them.

The celestial bodies are of two principal kinds; those, like the sun, which are composed of liquid incandescent masses; and those, like the outer planets of our system, which are so saturated with water at the temperature of spatial cold (273° below zero) that they are practically balls of ice. The inner planets of our system, Mercury, Venus, Mars, the Moon and the Earth, are composed of the same cosmic material as the fixed stars and the sun and, with the

253

exception of the earth, they are encased in shoreless ice-bound oceans. The earth alone has an atmosphere to prevent the oceans from freezing.

According to Glacial Cosmogony the moon, a metallo-mineral body covered with an ice-coat over 135 miles thick, was not, as orthodox selenology teaches, the child of our own earth in its liquid incandescent days, but an independent planet captured out of space by the earth and forced to become its satellite.

It is this process, the capture of satellites out of space and especially the capture of our present moon (for we have had six moons!) which concerns Atlantis.

Moon capturing is the inevitable result of the clockwork of a solar system. We have to imagine a great number of celestial bodies whirling round the sun. The hydrogen resistance of space gradually causes their orbits to decrease so that they are all spiralling towards the great gravitational centre of the sun. But they do not all close in upon the centre at the same speed. The larger bodies, the planets, offer greater resistance than the small ones to the coercive force of the hydrogen and the spin in finer spirals. The small bodies tend to reach the sun quicker, spinning faster and faster in rapidly decreasing spirals. Propelled by cosmic forces into the outskirts of a solar system, the orbit of a small body must in time "trespass" upon the orbit of larger bodies between it and the sun; but as their orbits approach each other the smaller body falls into the gravitational field of the larger, and, pulled out of its previous orbital course in relation to the sun, begins to spin round its captor instead. This capture invariably takes place when the stronger body is at the point of its orbit furthest from the sun and the weaker at its nearest.

The relations between the earth and the predecessor of our present moon must have been somewhat as follows. The process represents the "cosmic destiny" of all the former moons, and in time the same fate will overtake our present satellite, with disastrous consequences for the earth and all life upon it.

The Tertiary moon was smaller than the present moon. After its capture it approached the earth quicker and by its force of attraction pulled the waters away from the poles towards the equatorial regions of the earth, forming a tide-girdle round the tropics; it also drew most of the atmosphere from the poles to the equator, and the consequent lack of atmospheric protection lowered the temperature of the arctic zones to that of spatial cold, causing an Ice Age.

Meanwhile, the moon's orbital speed increased as it approached the earth until, at a distance of seven earth radii, the "month" (a complete circuit of the earth) and the "day" became the same length; in other words the moon took the same time to revolve round the earth as the earth to rotate once. The moon became "anchored" directly above the largest tract of tropical land, which was Africa. But it did not remain over exactly the same spot. Though it was motionless longitudinally, the angle formed by its orbit and the earth's equator daily caused a slight pendulum movement in the latitudinal sense.

At this period of the stationary moon, its attraction was so great that it broke the earth's tide-girdle and pulled that part of the earth which was directly beneath it right out of shape until both the globe and its atmosphere were distended roughly into the form of the point of an egg; the concentration of the atmosphere in the tropics increased the glacial movement at the poles, and the glaciers were drawn out into great tongues, stretching from the arctic regions right into the torrid zone. Meanwhile the daily pendulum movement of the satellite drew enormous seas which were concentrated beneath it to north and south. Mountainous floods swept all the loose material from the continents and scooped up the mud deposits of the previous age. Animals and plants were caught up in the swirling turbid waters and carried north and south towards the poles; there the foremost flood-waters froze before the ebb began and, when they rolled back in obedience to the swing of the planet, they left layer upon layer of congealed matter, animal, vegetable and mineral. In the course of time the weight of these accumulated layers melted the ice and pressed strata together, starting sliding glacier-like movements which distorted the once simple layer structure into complicated and fantastic formations. Thus, each succeeding lunar cataclysm is represented in the stratified rocks. This is the "tale of the rocks" by which geologists write the history of the earth, but according to Glacial Cosmogonists the rocks tell a very different story.

The Tertiary satellite did not, however, remain "station-ary" for long. It broke free from its "anchorage" and started to revolve round the earth faster than the earth itself could rotate. The orbital speed increased until, when it was at a distance of only $2\frac{R}{10}$ earth-diameters from the earth, it completed the circuit three times daily and there were thus three daily eclipses of the sun and moon.

The end came when the surface of the satellite was only 3,000 miles distant from the nearest point on the earth. Under the terrific disruptive force of the earth's gravitational pull the moon began to disintegrate. Upon the earth there first descended a terrible spiral hailstorm, consisting of great blocks of ice torn off the outer crust and accompanied with floods of water. As the moon's crust of ice peeled off and the inner layers of soil began to break up, the rain and hail turned to mud and stones and there were "showers of blood"; lastly the mineral core of the satellite disintegrated, metal fragments flew off it and came raining down upon the earth as great glowing meteorites which plunged thousands of feet below the earth surface. When the metal storm ceased, the Tertiary moon was gone.

So perished our last satellite; and the terror wrought in the mind of man by the final stages of its destruction, the monstrous disk blotting out the sky, the daily eclipses, the terrible earthquakes and floods, are reflected in the *Apocalypse* of St. John the Divine and the great *Ragnorok* story of the Norse Edda, which tells the story of a cataclysm so universal that even the gods were destroyed. Some

R

witnesses at any rate must have survived to tell the tale, living through it all in the safety of caves in the mountain tops. But this was the first of the great lunar cataclysms which man was able to record.

The Tertiary moon being no more, the subsequent history of the earth up till the time of the capture of our present moon, was one of reconstruction and the building up of great civilizations as the earth gradually returned to normal. The atmosphere once more enveloped the whole earth and under its temperate influence the glaciers retreated to the poles; the tide-girdle was no longer held in place by the pull of the satellite and its waters began to seek their true basins again; the flooded continental areas were gradually drained. Civilization started.

But the earth had only a relatively long period of peace. In Quaternary times we captured another satellite, the present moon. Mr Bellamy gives a graphic description of the capture and its effect upon the earth.

"The gravitational powers of the new satellite played freely upon the planet. They were very strong because they were fitful and jerky, as the moon approached very close during its perigees during the first 'months.'

"They wrenched the geoid out of shape and made the equator bulge out, more than it normally would for rotational reasons. This caused terrible earthquakes to shake the whole planet; it opened cracks in the earth's surface, along which seismic activity is still remarkably great; the greater part of our present active, and recently extinct, volcanoes came into existence then; the Niagara and Victoria Falls, and others, were formed then."

They also drew part of the atmosphere away from the poles. This caused the sudden great climatic breakdown which is supposed to have begun some 12,000 to 14,000 years ago.

"But the most important influence of the lunar gravitation was upon the waters. They yielded easily and fully to the satellite's pull, and streamed into the tropics. There they piled up a tide-girdle, a phenomenon which has not been recognized until now."

"In the pre-lunar aeon the distribution of land and water was different. The ancient outline of seas and continents is only preserved between the latitudes of about 35° to 40° north and south. The farther north and south we go from these narrow girdles, the higher the sea level was formerly, as we can gather from the still distinguishable ancient strand lines. The waters, withdrawn from the two vast callottes, suddenly surged, in a series of wild ring-waves, into the tropics, and submerged extensive land areas there. It is true, we cannot follow up the ancient shore-line beneath the waves, but we can form an idea of the extent and situation of the pre-lunar land areas from various evidences. For instance, the Congo Fiord allows us to guess at the original western margin of Africa, while the lumps of vitreous lava, fetched up by the dredge from the bottom of the mid-Atlantic, prove that parts of what is now sea must have been once land.

"When the planet Luna was captured, the realm of Atlantis met its sudden end; Lemuria disappeared; and the land of which Easter Island is the lone and enigmatic remainder was lost. The peoples that lived in the vast basin now occupied by the Mediterranean were wiped out. All over the earth there was a great setback in the progress of culture and civilization; everywhere man retrogressed, even to the tool-less age."

The tradition of the catastrophe of Atlantis, according to Mr Bellamy, is not preserved by Plato alone. The 17th and 18th chapters of *Revelations*, which refer to the downfall of Babylon, should be taken to refer to Atlantis; and he als sees references to Atlantis in *Jeremiah I* and *II*, and in the Tyrus passages in *Ezekiel*. He accepts Plato's story without reserve and also seems to accept the authenticity of the Le Plongeon interpretation of the famous Codex Troano, the Mayan pictographic MS. mentioned in the Schliemann document. But whatever the value of Glacial Cosmogony as a scientific theory Mr Bellamy presents a cosmic drama that is extremely impressive.

Appendix C

CLASSICAL TESTS RELEVANT TO ATLANTEAN THEORIES

Herodotus Book IV (Trans. G. L. Macaulay)

178   Next after the Lotophagoi along the sea coast are the Machlyans who also make use of the lotus, but less than those above mentioned. They extend to a river named the river Triton, and this runs out into a great lake called Tritonis, in which there is an island called Phla . . . The

179   following story moreover is also told, namely that Jason, when the *Argo* had been completed by him under Mount Pelion, put into it a hetacomb and with it also a tripod of bronze, and sailed round Peloponnese, desiring to come to Delphi . . . a north wind seized his ship and carried it off to Libya, and before he caught sight of land he had come to be in the shoals of the Lake Tritonis. Then as he was at a loss how he should bring his ship, the story goes that Triton appeared to him and bade Jason give him the Tripod, saying that he would show them the right course and let them go away without hurt: and when Jason consented to it he showed them the passage out between the shoals and set the Tripod in his own temple. . . .

180   They say moreover that Athene is the daughter of Poseidon and of the Lake Tritonis . . .

184   . . . Near this salt hill is a mountain named Atlas, which

261

is small in circuit and rounded on every side; and so exceedingly lofty is it said to be, that it is not possible to see its summits, for clouds never leave them either in the summer or in the winter. This, the natives say, is the pillar of the heaven. After this mountain these men got their name, for they are called Atlanteans; and it is said that they neither eat anything that has life nor have any dreams.

185   As far as these Atlanteans I am able to mention in order the names of those who are settled in the belt of sand; but for the parts beyond these I can do so no more. However, the belt extends as far as the Pillars of Hercules and also in the parts outside them. . . .

Diodorus Siculus Book III (Trans. C. H. Oldfather. Loeb Classical Library)

54   Setting out from the city of Chersonesus (states Dionysius of Mytilene,*) the Amazons embarked on great adventures, a longing having come over them to invade many parts of the inhabited world. The first people against whom they advanced, according to the tale, was the Atlanteans, the most civilized men among the inhabitants of those regions, who dwelt in a prosperous country and possessed great cities; it was among them, we are told, that

---

* III, 66. "This writer has composed an account of Dionysius and the Amazons, as well as the Argonauts and the events connected with the Trojan War and many other matters in which he cites the versions of the ancient writers, both the composers of myths and the poets."
    According to Dr Smith's *Dictionary of Greek and Roman Biography and Mythology*, Dionysius of Mitylene seems to have lived shortly before the time of Cicero, though he has been placed much earlier. His Argonautica, referred to by Appollonius Rhodius and Diodorus Siculus is not extant.

mythology places the birth of the gods, in the regions which lie along the shore of the ocean, in this respect agreeing with those among the Greeks who relate legends . . .

Now the queen of the Amazons collected, it is said, an army of 30,000 foot soldiers and 3,000 cavalry . . . For protective devices they used the skins of large snakes, since Libya contained such animals of incredible size, and for offensive weapons, swords and lances; they also used bows and arrows, with which they struck not only when facing the enemy but also when in flight, by shooting back at their pursuers with good effect. Upon entering the land of the Atlanteans they defeated in a pitched battle the inhabitants of the city of Cerne, as it is called, and working their way inside the walls along with the fleeing enemy, they got the city into their hands and desiring to strike terror into the neighbouring peoples they treated the captives savagely, put to the sword the men from the youth upward, led into slavery the women and children, and razed the city. But when the terrible fate of the inhabitants of Cerne became known among their fellow tribesmen, it is related that the Atlanteans, struck with terror, surrendered their cities on terms of capitulation and announced that they would do whatever should be commanded them, and that the Queen Myrina, bearing herself honourably towards the Atlanteans, both established friendship with them and founded a city to bear her name in place of the city which had been razed; and in it she settled both the captives and any native who so desired. Whereupon the Atlanteans presented her with

263

magnificent presents and by public decree voted to her notable honours, and she in return accepted their courtesy and in addition promised that she would show kindness to their nation. And since the natives were often being warred upon by the Gorgons, as they were named, a folk which resided upon their borders, and in general had that people lying in wait to injure them, Myrina, they say, was asked by the Atlanteans to invade the land of the afore-mentioned Gorgons. But when the Gorgons drew up their forces to resist them a mighty battle took place in which the Amazons, gaining the upper hand, slew great numbers of their opponents and took no fewer than 3,000 prisoners; and since the rest had fled for refuge into a certain wooded region, Myrina undertook to set fire to the timber, being eager to destroy the race utterly, but when she found that she was unable to succeed in her attempt she retired to the borders of her country.

55 Now as the Amazons, they go on to say, relaxed their watch during the night . . . the captive women . . . slew many of them; in the end, however . . . the prisoners fighting bravely were butchered one and all. Myrina accorded a funeral to her fallen comrades in three pyres and raised up three great heaps of earth as tombs, which are called to this day "Amazon Mounds." But the Gorgons, grown strong again in later days, were subdued a second time by Perseus, the son of Zeus, when Medusa was queen of them; and in the end both they and the race of the Amazons were entirely destroyed by Hercules when he

visited the regions to the west and set up his pillars in Libya* since he felt that it would ill accord with his resolve to be the benefactor of mankind if he should suffer any nations to be under the rule of women. The story is also told that the marsh Tritonis disappeared from sight in the course of an earthquake when those parts of it which lay towards the ocean were torn asunder.

56   But since we have made mention of the Atlanteans, we believe that it will not be inappropriate in this place to recount what their myths relate about the genesis of the Gods, in view of the fact that it does not differ greatly from the myths of the Greeks. Now the Atlanteans, dwelling as they do in the regions on the edge of the ocean and inhabiting a fertile territory, are reported far to excel their neighbours in reverence towards the Gods and the humanity they showed in their dealings with strangers . . . Their first King was Uranus, and he gathered the human beings, who dwelt in scattered habitations, within the shelter of a walled city . . . He also subdued the larger part of the inhabited earth, in particular the regions to the west and north. . . .

60   After the death of Hyperion, the myth relates, the kingdom was divided among the sons of Uranus, the most renowned of whom were Atlas and Cronus. Of these sons Atlas received as his part the regions on the coast of the ocean, and he not only gave the name of Atlanteans to his

*cf. IV, 18. When Hercules arrived at the farthest points of the continents of Libya and Europe he decided to set up these pillars to commemorate his campaign.

peoples but likewise called the greatest mountain in the land Atlas.

Book V, 19
(From Hoefer's *Bibliothèque Historique*. Paris 1846).

Having spoken of the islands situated on this side of the Pillars of Hercules we shall now describe those which are in the ocean. Towards Libya in the open sea there is an island, of considerable extent, and situated in the ocean. It is several days sail west of Libya, fertile, mostly mountainous and very beautiful. It is irrigated by navigable rivers, and there you can see numerous gardens planted with all sorts of trees, and orchards containing springs of soft water. . . . The mountainous region is covered with thick woods and fruit trees of all kinds. . . . The whole island is watered by soft springs which help to make the inhabitants both healthy and energetic. They hunt many different kinds of animal. . . . The climate is so temperate that tree-fruits and other produce grow abundantly for the greater part of the year. The island is so beautiful that it is more like a dwelling of the Gods than of men.

Aelian. *Various History*. III, 18
(From Dacier, *Aelianus, Histoires Diverses*. Paris 1772).

If we are to believe Theopompus, Midas, King of Phrygia, one day had a conversation with Silenus. (Silenus was the son of a nymph, and so, although he was born inferior to the God, he was nevertheless immortal and considerably above human beings). After speaking about various things, Silenus said to Midas:

"Europe, Asia and Libya are islands washed on every side by the ocean waves. Beyond the boundary of this world there is only one continent, of enormous size. It produces huge animals and men twice the stature of ours, who live twice as long. There are great cities governed according to their own unique custom, their laws forming a complete contrast with ours. Of these cities two are prodigiously large and quite different from each other. One is called Machimos (the Warlike) and the other Eusebia (the Pious). The Eusebians live in peace and abundance: the earth lavishes her fruits upon them; they have no need of carts and oxen, and it would be idle to work or sow the ground. After a life completely free from maladies, they remain gay and laughing; and their life is so pure that often the Gods do not bother to visit them.

The Machimos, on the other hand, are extremely warlike: always armed, always fighting, they toil ceaselessly to extend their boundaries. Here their city had become head of several nations: the population is not less than 2,000,000. . . . They have a great quantity of gold and silver which is less precious to them than iron is to us.

Once, continued Silenus, they wanted to penetrate into our island; and after crossing the ocean with 2,000,000 men, they reached the country of the Hyperboreans. But to their eyes this people appeared so vile and so contemptible that, having ascertained that it was nevertheless the happiest nation of our latitudes, they disdained to pass beyond.

Silenus went on to add even more astonishing information. In this land, he said, there were people called Meropes, masters of several great towns. On the borders of their territory is a place called Arroste (No Return), which is like a gulf, neither light nor dark. The air which forms its atmosphere is dark red. Two rivers flow about it. The River of Joy, and the River of Sorrow, they are called; their banks are covered with trees, the height of a tall plane tree. . . ."

Those who consider Theopompus of Chios as a trustworthy writer may believe this story. For my part, in this story and in several others, I can only see a writer of fairy tales.

Aelian. *De Natura Animalium* XV, 2.
(From Gk. and Lat. text. ed. Hercher, 1858).

The sea rams, of which many have heard tell but few know the natural history, except in so far as it is depicted in paintings and reliefs, winter in the straits between Corsica and Sardinia. They are seen standing right up above the surface of water, and the largest dolphins swim round them. The head of the male sea ram is bound with a white band, like the diadem, one might say, of Lysimachus or Antigonus or some other Macedonian King. The female sea ram actually has a tuft of hair hanging beneath her neck, like the little beards of cocks. Both these kinds feed on dead bodies, but they seize living bodies too

Appendix C

. . . Dwellers by the ocean tell the story that the ancient kings of Atlantis who traced their descent from Poseidon, wore head-bands of the skin of male sea rams, as a sign of authority. The queens likewise wore fillets of the female sea ram. . . .

Plutarch. *On the Face which appears on the Orb of the Moon*
(Trans. O. A. Prickard, 1911)

xxvi. I had scarcely finished speaking when Sylla broke in; "Stop Lamprias, and shut the door on your oratory, lest you run my myth aground before you know it, and make confusion of my drama, which requires another stage and a different setting. Now I am only its actor, but I will first, if you see no objection, name the poet, beginning in Homer's words:

Far o'er the brine an isle Ogygian lies (Od. vii, 244) distant from Britain five days sail to the west. There are three other islands equidistant from Ogygia and from one another, in the general direction of the sun's summer setting. The natives have a story that in one of these Cronus has been confined by Zeus, but that he, having a son for jailor, is left sovereign lord of those islands and of the sea, which they call the Gulf of Cronus. To the great continent by which the ocean is fringed is a voyage of about 5,000 stades, made in rowboats from Ogygia, or less from the other islands, the sea being slow of passage and full of mud because of the number of streams which the great mainland discharges, forming alluvial tracts and making

269

the sea heavy like land, whence an opinion prevailed that
it is actually frozen. The coasts of the mainland are inhabited by Greeks living round a bay as large as the Maeotic,
with its mouth nearly opposite that of the Caspian Sea. . . .
The natural beauty of the isle is wonderful and the mildness
of the environing air . . . Cronus himself sleeps within a
deep cave resting on rock which looks like gold, this sleep
being devised for him by Zeus in place of chains. Birds fly
in at the topmost part of the rock, and bear him ambrosia,
and the whole island is pervaded by the fragrance shed
from the rock as out of a well. The Spirits of whom we
hear serve and care for Cronus, having been his comrades
in the time when he was really king over gods and men.
Many are the utterances which they give forth of their own
prophetic power, but the greatest and those about the
greatest issues they announce when they return as dreams
of Cronus; for the things which Zeus premeditates, Cronus
dreams, when sleep has stirred the Titanic motions and
stirrings of the soul within him, and that which is royal and
divine alone remains, pure and unalloyed. . . ."

NOTES

Abbreviations.

U.H.W.=Universal History of the World.

J.H.S.=Journal of Hellenic Studies.

C.A.H.=Cambridge Ancient History.

Introduction.

1. T. A. Joyce. U.H.W.

2. Roger Devigne. "Trois Années d'activité de la 'Société d'Etudes Atlantéennes.'" In *L'Atlantide, exposé des hypothèses relatives à l'énigme d L'Atlantide*, trans. from the German of Alexander Bessmertny by F. Gidon, Paris, 1935.

3. Hindu, Madras, quoting Christian Science Monitor, Jan. 1936.

4. Dr Le Plongeon's theory was poetised by his wife in *Queen Moo's Talisman*, 1902. The poem describes the fatal rivalry of two brothers in love with their sister, Moo of Chichen, and the tragic destiny of the Can dynasty. At the beginning of the poem, Cay, the High Priest, unfolds to young Moo the tale of the destruction of the great land Mu, whence her ancestors came.

> In cities rich and great the housetops swarmed
> With frantic men, by fear to brutes transformed.
> Around the blackened, angry waters surged
> Till dwellings rocked, and melting soon were merged,
> Engulfed in dark abyss with writhing woe,
> All swiftly spent in one last awful throe!

*   *   *   *

Above the horrid sights and awful fear
Dark waters rolled, mud-laden many a year.
At dawn high crested waves, victorious
Exulted over Mu long glorious!

5. In a letter to Alexander Bessmertny.

6. Bessmertny. *L'Atlantide.* p. 187.

The Story of Atlantis.

1. A. E. Taylor. Plato. Ch. xvii.

2. A. E. Taylor.

3. See also *Republic* 10. Here Plato argues that the poets should be banished from the ideal state on the absurd grounds that the emotional effect of poetry is enervating to the public morale.

4. It has been suggested that Shakespeare himself was thinking of Atlantis, when he created Prospero's island, a possibility which might commend itself to Baconians, since Francis Bacon in his *New Atlantis* appears to have believed in the reality of Atlantis. But unfortunately for the Baconians he identifies it with America.

5. Bessmertny follows Schliermacher in stating this possibility. P. Couissin says (p. 130 *L'Atlantide de Platon*, 1928); "ce qui impressionne les géologues . . . c'est uniquement la coincidence des lieux . . . c'est tout-de-même étonnant, pensent-ils; Platon place son île dans l'Atlantique, précisément au même endroit que nous trouvons les traces d'un continent disparu."

6. For the fullest statement of the case against Atlantis, see P. Couissin, supra.

7. T. R. Glover. *Herodotus*. p. 133–134.

8. Despite Sir Thomas Browne's dry comment. "Of Alcinous his garden we read nothing beyond figs, apples and olives; if we allow it to be more than a fiction of Homer unhappily placed in Corfu, where the sterility of the soil makes men believe that there was no such thing at all."

9. J. L. Myres. *The Minoans and Micenae*. U.H.W. p. 786

10. K. T. Frost. *The Critias and Minoan Crete*. J.H.S. Vol. 33.

11. Sir Arthur Evans. *Palace of Minos*. Vol. IV, p. 192, 1935.

12. J. L. Myres. U.H.W. p. 942.

13. J.H.S. Vol. 33.

14. The Cretan source of Scheria was first suggested by Dr Drerup Homer, p. 130–135 and later the suggestion was elaborated by Dr Burrows. *The Discoveries of Crete* 1907. Dr Burrows considered that the Phaeacians themselves, the mariners, artists, feasters and dancers were the most obviously Minoan features of the story.

15. J.H.S. Vol. 33, p. 197.

16. Ibid, p. 203

17. Sir Arthur Evans. *Palace of Minos*. Vol IV, p. 943.

18. The trend of modern scholarship tends to justify this assumption.

19. E. A. Gardner. *Greeks in the Heroic Age*. U.H.W.

20. Though Homer does not actually state that Scheria is an island this is the opinion of most scholars; it is described as "in the sea."

S

21. *Herodotus* viii, 168. *Thucydides*, i, 111. *Strabo*, vi, 269; vii, 329.

22. A. Shewan. *Homeric Essays*. 1935.

23. *Antiquity*, Vol. X, no. 39, p. 38.

24. Schulten, Hennig, Jessen principally.

25. see p. 145.

26. Stanley Casson. *Cretan and Trojan Emigrés*. Classical Review, Vol. XLIV, 1930.

27. A. Shewan. *Homeric Essays*.

28. Lewis Spence. *The Problem of Atlantis*, p. 207.

29. P. Friedländer. *Platon. Eidos. Padaea. Dialogos. Excursus II*.

30. A. E. Taylor. *Plato's Timaeus and Critias*, p. 104.

31. Rivaud. *Platon. Oeuvres Complétes*. Vol. 10.

32. Bessmertny. *L'Atlantide*. p. 193.

33. C.A.H. Vol. IV, p. 536.

34. Saloman Reinach. *Orpheus*.

35. Rivaud. *Platon* X, 25.

36. C.A.H. IV, 532.

37. Sir J. G. Frazer. *Golden Bough*. Abridged Edition, p. 501.

38. This theory was first propounded by Bartoli in 1780, and was supported by Latreille in 1829. Taylor agrees.

39. Both Cervantes and Fielding thought that an epic theme could be developed in prose as well as in verse. W. P. Ker. *Form and Style in Poetry*.

40. "The connection of epic poetry with history is real, and it is a fitting subject for historical enquiry, but it lies

behind the scene. The epic poem is cut loose and set free from history, and goes on a way of its own." W. P. Ker. *Epic and Romance.*

41. Gilbert Murray. *The Rise of the Greek Epic.*

42. Ibid., p. 206.

43. Jowett. Trans. of *Critias* and *Timaeus*, with Commentary.

44. An interesting footnote to Professor Lowes' *The Road to Xanadu* deserved to be quoted in full.

"There is a singular coincidence to which Henri Cordier has called attention in his edition of *Cathay and the way thither*. In a 13th century account of Xaindu (Shangtu) which was not translated into any occidental language until years after Coleridge had dreamed his dream, occurs this statement. 'On the eastern side of that city a karsi or palace was built called Langtin, after a plan which the Khan had seen in a dream and retained in his memory.' In ancient tradition the stately pleasure-dome of Kubla Khan itself came into being, like the poem, as the embodiment of a remembered vision in a dream."

45. Among others which may have affected our knowledge of Atlantis is the collection of pictographic MSS. belonging to the ancient Aztec temples, destroyed by Juan de Zumarraga, first bishop of Mexico.

For a complete list see H. S. Bellamy. *Moons, Myths and Man*, 1936. Ch. "Lost archives of the world."

Through a Glass Darkly.

1. Paul Couissin. *L'Atlantide de Platon.*

2. See *Purchas His Pilgrimes*, Glasgow, 1906. XV, p. 235 The modern Aztla is about 100 miles from the Gulf of Mexico.

3. *Cambridge History of English Literature.* IV, 73.

4. M. Gautier. University of Algiers. *American Geographical Review*, 1926.

5. Ibid, 1934.

6. Each of them has accumulated quite a literature of its own, and the majority are well documentated and sufficiently current to deserve more detailed consideration than is possible here. The field of Atlantean researches is very adequately surveyed in Alexander Bessmertny's excellent book, *Das Atlantis-Rätsel*, Munich, 1933, available in the French translation of Dr F. Gidon, whose own theory of Atlantis forms an appendix to the French edition.

7. In *Atlantis in America*, Lewis Spence gives the following simple outline of geological time to assist the non-scientific reader to follow the evidence.

Primary or Palaeozoic Period—(Earliest forms of life).

Secondary or Mesozoic Period—(Reptilia, birds).

Tertiary Period—Early Tertiary, divided into: Palaeocene (Mammals); Eocene (Higher mammals); and Oligocene (Anthropoids). Late Tertiary, divided into: Miocene; and Pliocene (Man).

Quaternary Period—Pleistocene or Ice Age, divided into: Glacial and Post-Glacial. The beginning of the Pleistocene Age, is for practical purposes, generally reckoned at about 500,000 years ago. It is only in the last 25,000 years of this period that any form approaching modern man is to be found in Europe. The second division of the Quaternary is the Holocene, or "recent."

8. On earthworms see *Illustrated London News*, October 3rd, 1936.

9. Spence's opinion of the high state of the Cro-Magnon civilization should, despite Sir Arthur Keith, be accepted with caution. In his desire to prove that the Atlanteans, though Stone Age men, were not mere savages, it is possible to detect another more naif motive which has already been mentioned as a common inspiration of Atlantean polemic. "If a patriotic Scotsman may be forgiven the boast, I may say that I devoutly believe that Scotland's admitted superiority in the mental and spiritual spheres springs almost entirely from the preponderance of Cro-Magnon blood which certainly runs in the veins of her people, whose height and cranial capacity as well as other physical signs, show them to be mostly of the Cro-Magnon race." Such lapses from the scientific approach to Atlantis are, however, much rarer in Spence's work than in that of the majority of Atlantean protagonists.

10. *Couvade.* "A term applied by some writers to the 'man childbed' attributed to some uncivilized or primitive races, and extended to comprehend a series of customs, according to which, on the birth of a child, the father performs acts or simulates states natural or proper to the mother, or abstains for a time from certain foods or actions, as if he were physically affected by the birth." *Oxford English Dictionary.*

11. G. Elliot-Smith. *Human History, p.* 489.

12. A. Kingsley Porter. *Legends and Crosses of Ireland,* p. 7.

13. E. K. Chambers. *Arthur of Britain.*

14. Donald Mackenzie. *Ancient Man in Britain,* p. 11.

15. According to T. D. Kendrick. *The Druids,* p. 57. "There is not a scrap of evidence suggesting any direct imposition of eastern Culture upon Gaul or Britain, and whatever cultural improvement came from such a source, *i.e.* from Mesopotamia or Egypt, must be attributed not to colonization, nor even to far-flung trade, but to the natural and inevitable *firebucket* progress of ideas, *culture-creep,* that all ages have witnessed . . . "

16. C. B. Lewis. *Classical mythology and Arthurian romance,* 1932.

17. *Antiquity,* March 1926.

18. W. Shepherd. *Armchair Science,* October, 1936.

19. H. G. Wells. *Short History of the World.*

20. J. W. Spencer. *Submarine valleys off the American coast and in the North Atlantic.* Bull. Geol. Soc. America, vol. XIV, p. 207, 1903.

21. E. Hull. *The suboceanic physiography of the North Atlantic ocean.* London, 1912.

22. Submarine Valleys. *Geographical Review,* Vol. XXIII. 1933.

23. *Geology and Paleontology of the Georges Bank Canyons.* Bull. Geol. Soc. America. Vol. XLVII, 1936.

24. Dr Leakey writes (*Early Man in Kenya,* 1935). "Our

survey of the human remains so far discovered in association with Stone Age cultures has shown us that true *Homo* has been present in Kenya from the beginning of the Pleistocene onwards, and further that a fully developed *Homo Sapiens* has been present since the early part of the middle Pleistocene." This indicates a date approximately 250,000 years ago.

Then Face to Face.
1. Lemuria was the name given to the hypothetical continent postulated by the German zoologist Haeckel in order to explain the distribution of lemurs!
2. Paul Brunton. *In search of Secret Egypt*, 1936.
3. Scott-Elliot. *The Story of Atlantis*, 1882.
4. *Gondwana land*, the name now given to a central tract of India, was a Pacific continent postulated by various zoologists and botanists to explain the distribution of flora and fauna. Lemuria, as conceived by the theosophists, seems to have been part of it. On the other hand, soundings of the Pacific completed in 1933 by Captain Claude Banks Mayo of the U.S. Navy show that there is a submerged continent, with mountains, river courses and plateaux at an average depth of one mile stretching from the Hawaiian to the Barin Islands, east of the coast of Japan. East of Hawaii the ocean floor drops to an even level of 3 miles all the way to the Californian coast.

Vast Shady Hills.
1. Dennis Saurat. *Blake and Modern Thought*, 1929.

2. For full information about Stukeley, see Mr Stuart Piggott's article in *Antiquity*, March 1935.

3. Lewis Spence. *History of Atlantis*, p. 35. Spence unfortunately does not quote his source.

4. Introduction. *Histoire Philosophique du Genre Humain.* Lib. Gén. des Sc. Occultes. Paris.

5. Dennis Saurat. *Blake and Modern Thought.*

Lost Dreams and Plaintive Hopes.

1. This and subsequent passages from the *Republic* are quoted from the translation of J. L. Davies and D. S. Vaughan, Macmillan, 1923.

2. E. O. Winstedt. *The Christian Topography of Cosmas Indicapleustes.*

3. Printed in 1866 under the title of *Traffic* in a volume called *A Crown of Wild Olives.*

4. Cecil Day Lewis. *From Feathers to Iron.* Hogarth Press.

5. Wyndham Lewis. *One Way Song.* Faber and Faber.

INDEX

Index

Index

THE NEWCASTLE FORGOTTEN FANTASY LIBRARY

THE GLITTERING PLAIN by William Morris is the first title in The Newcastle Forgotten Fantasy Library, a new series of 26 adult fantasy classics. The works of William Morris (1834-1896) have influenced many writers of fantasy, such as Lord Dunsany, C.S. Lewis, and J.R.R. Tolkien, and continue to delight new generations of readers with their flights of high adventure in strange lands, their beautiful maidens and stalwart heroes. THE STORY OF THE GLITTERING PLAIN was the first of these romances. A must for the millions of Tolkien fans!

174 Pages   5½ x 8½ $2.45

THE SAGA OF ERIC BRIGHTEYES by H. Rider Haggard is a masterpiece of heroic fantasy by the creator of "SHE" and "KING SOLOMON'S MINES." No. 2 in the Newcastle Library of Forgotten Fantasy Classic Series. H. Rider Haggard achieved phenomenal popularity in his own day as a writer of fantastic romances and adventure tales, but today many of his lesser known works are all but forgotten. Such a novel is ERIC BRIGHTEYES, an heroic saga of bold adventure, treachery and dark sorcery. Haggard's biographer, Morton Cohen, said of ERIC BRIGHTEYES, "It is one of his best!" Illustrated.

304 Pages   5½ x 8½ $2.95

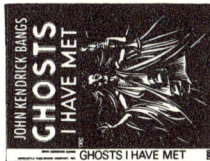

GHOSTS I HAVE MET Edited by John Kendrick Bangs. Here is a delightful collection of classic ghost stories by a master humorist. Here are spectres to make you smile instead of shiver, gleeful ghosts, amusing apparitions, and humorous haunts. Long out-of-print, this new edition of GHOSTS I HAVE MET, by the author of A HOUSE BOAT ON THE STYX is an unabridged reproduction of the 1898 edition, with all the original illustrations by Peter Newell, A.B. Frost and Richards.

191 Pages   5½ x 8½ $2.45

OTHER QUALITY PAPERBACKS BY NEWCASTLE

The Newcastle Forgotten Fantasy Library

F-100	THE GLITTERING PLAIN by Wm. Morris	$2.45	
F-101	THE SAGA OF ERIC BRIGHTEYES		
	by H. Rider Haggard	$2.95	

Self-Enrichment Books

W-22	MARRIAGE COUNSELING: Fact or Fallacy		
	By Jerold R. Kuhn	$2.95	
H-21	VIEWPOINT ON NUTRITION		
	By Arnold Pike	$2.95	
S-2	LOVE, HATE, FEAR, ANGER		
	and the other lively emotions By June Callwood	$2.45	
G-6	IMPORTANCE OF FEELING INFERIOR		
	By Marie Beynon Ray	$2.95	
S-0	FORTUNATE STRANGERS		
	By Cornelius Beukenkamp, Jr.,M.D.	$2.95	
G-9	THE CONQUEST OF FEAR By Basil King	$2.95	
H-4	YOU ARE WHAT YOU EAT By Victor H. Lindahr	$2.25	
D-11	VITAMIN COOKBOOK By Victor H. Lindahr	$2.95	
H-15	EAT AND REDUCE By Victor H. Lindahr	$2.45	
H-16	ROMANY REMEDIES AND RECIPES		
	By Gipsy Petulengro	$2.25	
H-17	THE NATURAL WAY TO HEALTH		
	By Victor H. Lindahr	$2.95	
G-20	THOUGHT VIBRATIONS By A. Victor Segno	$2.45	

Occult Books

W-1	RITUAL MAGIC By E. M. Butler	$3.45	
P-12	NUMEROLOGY MADE PLAIN		
	By Ariel Yvon Taylor	$2.45	
P-3	MAGIC, WHITE AND BLACK		
	By Franz Hartmann, M.D.	$3.45	
P-5	GHOSTS I HAVE MET By John Kendrick Bangs	$2.45	
P-10	BOOK OF DREAMS AND GHOSTS		
	By Andrew Lang	$2.95	
P-8	THE DEVIL IN BRITAIN AND AMERICA		
	By John Ashton	$3.75	
P-14	AN INTRODUCTION TO ASTROLOGY		
	By William R. Lilly	$3.75	
T-7	FORTUNE TELLING FOR FUN By Paul Showers	$2.95	
W-13	ORIGINS OF POPULAR SUPERSTITIONS AND		
	CUSTOMS By T. Sharper Knowlson	$2.95	
P-19	PRACTICAL ASTROLOGY		
	By Connie C. de Saint-Germain	$2.95	
P-18	THE PRACTICE OF PALMISTRY		
	By Connie C. de Saint-Germain	$3.95	
P-23	LOST ATLANTIS by James Bramwell	$3.45	
G-24	GRAPHOANALYSIS by William L. French	$2.95	
P-25	THIRTY YEARS AMONG THE DEAD		
	by Car. A. Wickland, M.D.	$3.95	

*Please check with your favorite Bookseller for any of the Books listed
on this page or order directly from:*

NEWCASTLE PUBLISHING COMPANY, INC.

1521 No. Vine St. Hollywood, California   90028

NOW *from*

NEWCASTLE

These 4 Bestselling Books

YOU ARE WHAT YOU EAT
$2.25

EAT AND REDUCE
$2.45

VITAMIN COOKBOOK
$2.95

THE NATURAL WAY TO HEALTH
$2.95

by Victor Lindlahr